From Good to Grace

Letting Go *of the* Goodness Gospel

Christine Hoover

BakerBooks

a division of Baker Publishing Group
Grand Rapids, Michigan

Published by Baker Books
a division of Baker Publishing Group
P.O. Box 6287, Grand Rapids, MI 49516-6287
www.bakerbooks.com

Printed in the United States of America

Library of Congress Cataloging-in-Publication Data
Hoover, Christine.
    From good to grace : letting go of the goodness gospel / Christine Hoover.
        pages cm
    Includes bibliographical references.
    ISBN 978-0-8010-1667-7 (pbk.)
    1. Christian women—Religious life. 2. Grace (Theology). I. Title.
BV4527.H663 2015
248.8′43—dc23   2014034559

15   16   17   18   19   20   21   7   6   5   4   3   2   1

"*From Good to Grace* is a song of freedom for the world-weary woman; for the believer who wonders if she'll ever feel good enough; for the single person, wife, or mother who longs to matter. It is the promise of an extraordinary life in an upside-down kingdom, a must-read in an age when the spirit of the church thirsts to be revived."

—**Emily T. Wierenga**, award-winning journalist, artist, and author of five books including the memoir *Atlas Girl: Finding Home in the Last Place I Thought to Look*

"Christine helps untangle the knots we can make of the gospel. With humble transparency and gifted clarity, she works out the kinks in our understanding of grace. This book is full of wisdom, and as you read it, your soul will breathe a deep sigh of relief. Jesus has accomplished for us far more than we often realize, and the results of his victory are liberating!"

—**Kelly Matte**, wife of Gregg Matte, pastor of Houston's First Baptist Church and founder of Breakaway Ministries at Texas A&M University

"Christine Hoover has a surprise for you. The surprise isn't something that can be bought, traded, or stolen. The surprise Christine offers comes from deep inside her heart as she lets her personal encounter with Jesus roll onto the printed pages of her book. Christine is passionate about encouraging women to live and lead from grace. Her new book, *From Good to Grace*, is a perfect title for the adventure of faith you will embrace through its pages. Her own words "I'm ordinary" help us as women relax and receive fresh insight that takes us from the Gospel of Goodness to the Gospel of Grace! Enjoy the journey. You will be blessed."

—**Pat Layton**, author of *Life Unstuck: Peace with Your Past, Purpose for Your Present, Passion for Your Future*

"Christine has written the book that I believe women in our generation are really dying to read. In a practical and honest way, she exposes the truth and lets God's grace do its very good work in our lives. This book has been a huge tool to help me stop shouting with a raspy and tired voice, 'I'm good! I'm good, aren't I?' and start looking to my very good God who covers me in his love."

—**Jess Connolly**, entrepreneur and author

To my boys, Will, Reese, and Luke,
because my greatest desire is for each of you
to receive and enjoy God's grace
and to respond to him with your lives

Contents

Part One Good, Bye

  1. Obsessed with Goodness   11
  2. The Most Important Things   29
  3. You Can't Go Back Again   43

Part Two From Good to Grace: *Receiving*

  4. Receiving His Love   69
  5. Receiving His Help   89
  6. Receiving His Freedom   111

Part Three From Good to Grace: *Responding*

  7. Love Shows   133
  8. Giving Grace   153
  9. We Hope   177

Contents

Conclusion: *We Will Live in Grace*   199

Acknowledgments   205

Discussion Guide   207

Notes   215

An Invitation   219

Part One

Good, Bye

Having begun in the Spirit, are you now being made
perfect by the flesh?

Galatians 3:3

1

Obsessed with Goodness

A S I PULLED JEANS in various sizes from the dryer, sorting
and stacking them into three neat piles representative of each
of my boys, I estimated how many times I'd done this exact task in
the previous twelve months. Perhaps 416 times? The number seemed
low, quite honestly, because I felt in that moment as if I'd spent
my entire life reaching into the dryer for one more pair of pants
with holes in the knees or one more pair of superhero underwear.
And what did it say about me that the most exciting purchase of
the year, a purchase I effused over to anyone who would listen for
months afterward, was a large-capacity washer and dryer? By my
gleeful estimation, that purchase had cut my time standing at the
washer and dryer by at least half.

My laundry calculations led to more: the number of peanut
butter and jelly sandwiches made, meals slaved over, noses wiped,

toilets cleaned, grocery stores conquered, and birthday parties planned.

Final tally: a lot.

I had been busy in the past year, not just with our boys and their myriad of needs and activities but also with ministry activities outside our home. As a pastor's wife, my opportunities had been plentiful for discipleship, counseling, leading, hosting, and planning, and I'd happily taken advantage of each one.

Final tally: a lot, a lot.

In that moment, standing at the washer and dryer, I wasn't grumbling to myself, as if the gifts of family and ministry weren't a blessing, or as if these opportunities were just tasks to me. I simply had a salient moment where I sat with the whole of my life in front of me and questioned if all those numbers and tasks and activities and relationships added up to my life counting for something. Was God using my life to impact others in meaningful ways?

What I really found myself asking was this: *Am I a good Christian, wife, mom, and minister?* Because that's what I want more than anything else—for my life to mean something in the kingdom of God, to be good at these things.

But I'm just making sandwiches.

I'm just hosting one of our church's small groups.

I'm just writing blog posts as a means of trying to make sense of what God is teaching me.

I'm just sewing a button on a shirt for my husband and saying a prayer for him as he stands to preach on Sunday mornings.

I'm just listening to a friend pour out her heart and trying to say the words that will help.

I don't necessarily feel that I'm making a huge dent in this world in the name of Jesus. I don't feel particularly good at anything, except maybe making to-do lists and getting overwhelmed at the number of demands on that list.

And although I don't feel particularly good at anything, I want *desperately* to be good at the things that matter most to me.

I want to be a good wife to a husband who is infinitely good to me. When he has a need, I want to meet it kindly and graciously. When we disagree, I want to respond with gentleness and patience. I want him to enjoy our marriage and be glad he chose me for life. Too often, however, I'm indifferent, distracted, or offering him only my leftover energy and attention. I want to be a good wife—but what is a good wife, exactly, and how do I become one?

I also very much want to be a good mom. And if there is one thing I want to do well with my kids, it's rearing them to know God's voice and love his ways. But if there is one area I feel most inadequate in, it's rearing my children to know God's voice and love his ways, and every other little thing I'm trying to teach them under this larger umbrella, whether it's tying shoes or polite social interactions or how to share with one another.

I panic when I think of my children embarking into adulthood, typically because I imagine that they'll have to call me to come tie their shoes or they'll freeze to death because I'm not there to remind them to wear pants and coats in the winter. Or they'll spend every waking minute in front of a video game console because I'm not there to monitor their activities. Will they ever walk with the Lord? Will they become leaders in their homes and influencers in their communities? Will they love people well?

And then I remember that a man isn't built in a day, and to keep my eyes in the moment, to take small steps, to do the next thing. But even for the moment, I often feel powerless and overcome by the mountain in front of me. I feel like I should be better at this than I am. Or maybe it's that I feel like all these things should come easily to a "good mother," so I must not be one. I *want* to be one. However, what exactly is a good mother and how do I become one?

I also very much want to be a good friend to the women I spend my life with. I want to have an abundance of energy and time and love to pour out on them. I want to remember their birthdays and give them delightful gifts and play fun games together while laughing boisterously late into the night. I want to let them see me cry and tell them when I need help rather than keeping it to myself because I don't want to be a burden. And I very much want them to feel free to cry on me and call on me. But the reality of it is that I am often in bed before nine, and I sometimes remember to get a birthday card, and I forget to follow up with friends on important conversations. I can be difficult to know. And I hurt people sometimes; I know I do. Despite it all, I want to be a good friend, but what exactly is a good friend and how do I become one?

I am so impatient with myself, so hard on myself, so quick to throw my hands up in frustration or surrender. I find myself thinking that God feels that same way toward me: impatient that I'm not further along, frustrated that I fail, irritated by my faithless worrying. Those thoughts reveal that I often perceive God as huffing at my weaknesses, wishing I could get it together already, arms crossed and foot tapping.

And this is, in fact, where I feel the most weight in my heart because, most of all, I want to please God. I want to be a good Christian. I desperately want to be good at the things that matter most to him. I want to be good at what he wants me to be good at and give myself to the things he wants me to give myself to. *And just what is that exactly?*

I Thought Life Would Be Glamorous

Maybe I overanalyze these things. Or maybe I'm making life harder than it's supposed to be. Either way, as I'm approaching middle age, I evaluate my life and the way I'm living it way more than I did when I was younger. I used to think about other things.

As I hoisted the laundry basket full of clean, folded clothes onto my hip, I thought about my younger self and the dreams I'd had for my life. In those days, I envisioned being a good Christian and living an impactful life would look a bit different than four-hundred-plus loads of laundry a year or stopping on the street to chat with a neighbor or preparing a simple meal for a new mom. An impactful life involved teaching a large Bible study, going places, or being known and admired by crowds of people, or . . . I don't know really what it is that I thought would make it all count for God. Something dramatic. Something glamorous. Something spectacular.

In college, I attended the first-ever Passion conference in Austin, Texas, with several thousand other students. The whole thing was life-changing in many ways, full of mind-searing moments. One such moment: Louie Giglio, exhorting us to be a generation that would live for God's renown, asked us to stand if we might be willing to die for Christ, to literally give our lives for him. I stood with others, agreeing that I would. And I meant it. I stood because I desperately wanted to be a good Christian and do big things for God, and I imagined that physical death on behalf of Christ was about the biggest thing I could possibly do for him. A moment of standing publicly for Jesus definitely fit the dramatic and spectacular mold.

It wasn't difficult to stand, however, because martyrdom was a lofty ideal for me; I doubted I would ever be asked to make good on that promise. However, I mentally made a list of additional "big things" I might consider in case the martyrdom thing didn't materialize: becoming a missionary or remaining single so I could serve Christ with an undivided focus. That was about all I could come up with, but, nonetheless, I assented in my heart to living a big life for God.

That's what I thought about as I put the laundry away: I had assumed that living life for God and being a good Christian would be a big, splashy to-do. In reality, I'm still waiting for God to ask me to do something "big." I am no longer single, but I sort of became a missionary when my husband and I parachute-dropped into a new city and started a church. I say "sort of" because I'm still living what feels like an average life of laundry, PTO, peanut butter and jelly sandwiches, superhero underwear, and church and community ministry. My view of the world-impacting person I would be as an adult involved a great deal more energy and discretionary time than I currently have, and now that I think about it, my future life involved comfort, ease, and plenty of applause too. My future self was really confident, was an excellent public speaker, was revered in the community, had the Bible memorized, and lived in a Pottery Barn–themed house. But in my current everyday life, I don't always feel like I'm getting it right. I don't walk around feeling super confident that I'm making a huge imprint on the world or anything. People don't part like the Red Sea when I walk around town, unless, of course, they are trying to avoid me because they know I'm the pastor's wife and that might make things a little awkward.

I'm ordinary.

My life doesn't look like what I imagined as an idealistic college student. I see weakness and failure in myself. I'm less confident than I was in college and, somehow, I know so much less than I did then. I've experienced wounds and dark days that I thought might incapacitate me once and for all. I'm tired a lot and don't love people like I should. I feel overwhelmed in parenting sometimes and I don't always feel like I'm a good pastor's wife or good just plain wife. My work is typing words on a page to encourage and help others, but most of the time it feels like I'm just processing a jumble of thoughts and emotions by spewing them out on paper. And then there are all the rote routines and inconsequential days, bills to pay, and deadlines to meet. How could I possibly be making an impact in the name of Christ when I'm not particularly fabulous at anything? Am I resigned to a minor part in God's story, or is this everyday life of small moments somehow adding up to a life that matters?

The State We're In

I know I'm not alone in this quiet desperation, because everywhere I turn I meet and engage with women who want to be good Christians and who want their lives to count for the kingdom of God, but they are often confused about how to do that and doubtful it will ever be a reality, because they're mostly weighed down with doubts and grief and life's unmet expectations. They are standing at the dryer, sitting at a desk, volunteering at church, cracking open their Bibles, or serving family or roommates in seemingly unseen ways, yet still waiting eagerly for the day when God asks them to do big things in his name or when they finally feel good enough to be used by him at all. The women I talk to are just like me, stumbling through singleness or marriage or careers or parenting, trying so hard to be good at it all.

Didn't Jesus talk about joy and purposefulness and the abundant life? There seems to be a great disconnect between the message of Jesus and our everyday lives.

In some ways, I believe this is because we can't often figure out what it is that God wants from us, or perhaps it's that we don't even think to ask him or to listen intently for his answer. So we go on doing what we think we *ought* to do, or what everyone else around us is doing. We create strategies, make to-do lists, choose activities, and organize ourselves within an inch of our lives based upon what we see online or what influential people tell us we should be doing. We're striving with everything in us toward goodness, toward making an impact, driven by the expectation of what our lives *should* look like.

Our ideas of pleasing God involve being good at everything, never having weaknesses or mess-ups, having every skill and gift, and keeping the religious plates spinning at all times. If we are good, we surmise, we'll be loved, we'll make a significant impact in the world, and God will be honored. And then we look around for results and ripples as evidence of how "good" we are and, tellingly, these evidences are usually external: well-behaved children, an adoring husband or a line of suitors, the admiration of other women, a job we love, a Pinterest-worthy home, a set of fun friends, and a comfortable life. In this paradigm, comparison and competition abound, and success is externally measured and only for a few. We are obsessed with goodness, and our addiction to it is growing in the age of the internet, where we can compare our goodness with others or add more to our "to-do" goodness list. But, if we're honest, when we live in this paradigm none of us really feel like we're doing enough.

The state we're in was on full display at a women's conference I attended recently. Just as the speaker took her place at the podium, the woman next to me slid her book across the table, offering me a quick peek inside. She said I could have it for free if I would promote it on my blog, so I politely flipped through the pages, glanced at the back cover, and set it on the table as I turned my attention to the stage. I became engrossed in the speaker's story, furiously writing down her hard-won wisdom, but to my left, the woman who had passed me her book pulled out her cell phone and began scrolling through her Facebook and Twitter feeds. I casually inched her book back to her side of the table, certain I would not read it or promote it because of *her*.

I did not know this woman and I may very well have completely misread her, but no matter because in that moment, that woman—seemingly so intent on promoting herself, so self-focused, so image-driven—raised a full-length mirror to my own heart. I was gripped by it, so sure of what I was seeing. She reflected back to me my own dark desires of instant success, popularity, and influence. I saw a clamorer, dissatisfied, concerned with worldly success more than character, concerned with making a self determined big splash for Jesus but wanting desperately to bypass daily faithfulness and dependence.

In the mirror, I saw wickedness.

I ran, ashamed, considering the core of the matter, the lies that weave their way into my life:

What I'm doing is not enough.

What I have is not enough.

I am not enough.

I am concerned about the state of my heart that gets so easily caught up in the online frenzy of self-promotion and image-keeping, or that gets wrapped in knots when conversations among women turn to their choices that have not been my own. I am concerned about all of us, that we are pining after, and comparing, and envying ourselves away. We are clamoring to stake out our place in the world, to be noticed or seen or loved or respected. We are so worried about being good we're losing our souls in the process.

In Christian culture, women feel great confusion and even pressure about what we should be doing and why we should be doing it. This confusion touches decisions about education, family, eating and drinking, work, hobbies, community involvement, and even whether one should volunteer when the sign-up sheet is passed around again at church. The pressure grows when choices are wrapped in spiritual or more-spiritual terms. We see it everywhere: Do something great! Follow your dreams! Make a difference for the kingdom! Be missional and in community! For the gospel-confused, that too often translates into: I'm not doing enough, what I'm doing isn't making a difference, and I've got to create my own and my neighbor's own and my children's own and everyone's own life transformation.

As a result, the Christian women I talk to feel distant from God, experience self-doubt, constantly compare themselves with other women, live hurried and overextended lives, and wonder desperately if they are "good" Christians who please God. I've been that woman, and I'm fighting not to be that woman now.

When I open my Bible and read the truth it offers, I don't see a correlation between this frantic pursuit of good and the way Jesus talked. He never patted anyone on the head and said, "What a good person you are. I'm so proud of you!" But isn't that what we're chasing, the "atta-girl" from Jesus? Might I be hard pressed to find people who claim Jesus who are living the abundant, light-yoked life he promised them? Do *I* live that way? And why are we not asking these questions?

When is enough, enough? When do we stop the self-made plans, the flow of information, the swirling thoughts, and the self-condemnation to ask the simple question, "What is it that *God* wants from us?"

As I put the superhero underwear away, stack by stack, I saw it. I know what *I* want for me: I want to be good. No, I'm *obsessed* with being good. I'm obsessed with external, circumstantial results that prove once and for all that I'm a good wife, mom, friend, and Christian. I'm creating a certain image of myself and doing things that *I* consider noteworthy. My concerns are self-focused concerns, not God-focused concerns. I am not living according to the very gospel that I claim.

And here I thought I was done with all that.

The Goodness Gospel

This is where I tell you my story, and this is mostly what you need to know to understand my story: I've been obsessed with being good and performing all my life.

Hello, my name is Christine. I'm a goodness addict

I was born with a list in my hand, or at least that's how early I imagine it started. I came by it honestly—my mom's response to everything my sister and I needed as children, whether shampoo from the store or help with a school project, was always, "Make a list!"

So I did. I made list after list—of library books for summer reading, of boys that I liked, of songs to record from the radio on my tape recorder, of necessities to pack for overnight camp, of must-haves in my future husband, even of outfits for the first month of eighth grade so as not to repeat and make a fashion faux pas of infinite proportion.

I don't just make lists. I am *that* person, the one who adds a task to a list just to experience the satisfaction of crossing it off, the one who makes lists for my lists.

I'm a perfectionist.

There was a time when I would have said that with pride, but not anymore. Perfectionism has not been a friend to me. Sure, my house is organized and my budget spreadsheet is up-to-date, but when perfectionism is applied to the spiritual needs of the heart, it's called legalism. And *legalism* is a fancy word for an obsession with goodness. It's a belief that good things come from God to those who are good. And it's a belief that you can actually be good enough to get to God on your own.

I became a Christian at age eight. From that point, or more accurately from the point in middle school when I started having "quiet times" according to my youth minister's instructions, until my late twenties, I spent the majority of my Christian life striving—striving for perfection, for God's favor, for the approval of others, and for the joy and freedom that the Bible spoke of yet completely eluded me.

It seemed to me that an endless to-do list had been delivered first-class to my doorstep the second I said the sinner's prayer.

And as I've already admitted, I'm pretty good at lists—or lists are pretty good at controlling me, one of the two. After I had been a Christian for a few years, God's to-do list, or at least the list I perceived him to have, kept growing like an unstoppable cancer not responding to treatment. "Read the Bible" became "Read the Bible every day," and then "Read the Bible every day for thirty minutes before school or else God is mad at you and Kirby will sneeze a snot rocket into the back of your hair again in geometry." I just knew if I could check off every item on the to-do list, I would be the model Christian and God would pat me on the back, winking like jolly old Santa Claus as he whispered, "I'm so glad you're on my team." Most importantly, my attempts at perfection would make him love me.

At an early age, I fell for perfectionism's lie that I could be good enough to win God's heart and the approval of others. I sought joy, peace, and love through being good, and instead found myself miserably enslaved to my own unattainable standards.

This was my understanding of what it meant to be a Christian: If I do good things, then God is pleased. If I do things wrong, then he is angry. This is actually the basis of every religion on earth *except* Christianity, this idea of a scale where the good must outweigh the bad in order to be right with God. I had religion down pat, but the religion I practiced wasn't true and biblical Christianity. On the outside I appeared to be a good Christian, but on the inside I felt unlovable and was riddled with guilt about my inability to please God.

Unfortunately for me, a large part of a goodness obsession is an addiction to self. Goodness is evaluated by activity, completed tasks, responses from others, and results. It requires a focus on appearance and image and maintaining some semblance of religious behavior. Goodness required that I control my environment with military precision, hide my weaknesses, and compare myself with others or my own arbitrary standards. Goodness fed both my pride and my self-condemnation and kept me relationally isolated.

The other part of a goodness addiction, I discovered in my twenties, is a faulty understanding of who God is and what he expects from his children. I only saw God through perfectionism's filter. He was gray. He had no patience for my mistakes, forever glaring at me with a scowl on his face. He sighed a lot. If I was extra good, he *might* manage to crack a smile. He was one-dimensional, disengaged, and unaffectionate, and I absolutely feared him.

I knew nothing about grace.

I knew nothing about forgiveness.

I knew nothing about the true gospel, because a goodness addiction completely overtakes the heart and mind, leaving no room for truth. It enslaves and cannibalizes itself. It becomes an all-encompassing religion, closing tightly around one's soul. It led me down paths of depression and despair.

And it became my gospel.

The True Gospel

I lived according to the goodness gospel for far too long.

But God pursued me. He used multiple people to reveal my goodness addiction and to show me both his true nature and the truth of what he had done for me at the cross, but he used my husband most of all.

About a year into our marriage, Kyle and I got into a life-changing fight. Can a fight be one-sided? Because that's what it was. I snapped at him about something trivial, and instead of snapping back, he just calmly left the room. I was being a crazy person and he knew it. As soon as he left, I felt ashamed. Why had I gotten so angry about something of such small consequence? Why would I choose to hurt my husband like that? With my tail between my legs, I went to him.

"I'm sorry," I said, pleading with my eyes for him to release me of what I'd done.

"I forgive you," he said, and he meant it. He actually smiled as he said it.

That's it? I thought. No penance required, no pouting, no silent treatment, no dumping on of shame, nothing? *It's just forgiven that easily?*

My eyes must have revealed my uncertainty because he reached out for my hand and pulled me to his lap. Then he wrapped his arms around me, looked me in the eyes, and reiterated, "I forgive you. I love you, Christine."

As we embraced, the Lord whispered to my heart, the heart deaf to true forgiveness and grace, *This is exactly how I love you. I don't keep a record of wrongs or hold your sin over your head. When you confess something to Me, I forgive you. I delight in you.*

At this point in our marriage and ministry, God, through the book of Galatians, had begun showing me how little I truly understood of the gospel. Instead of the true gospel, I was living by what Paul called the "perverted" gospel, one of works and dead religion. My heart and mind were starting to wake up to the truth because my husband had become a pastor, and our new ministry life was shining a very bright light on my self-sufficiency and attempts at self-justification. I discovered quickly that I could not meet ministry's demands—and I certainly could not love—according to bootstrap religion.

The beacon of light, simultaneously convicting and life-giving, was Galatians 5:4: "You have become estranged from Christ, you who attempt to be justified by law." That is exactly how I felt—like an outsider standing apart from Christ, nose plastered to the glass, trying desperately to earn my belonging. At the same time, I rejected any of Christ's advances toward me out of shame over my failures and out of my stubborn self-determination.

This passage described how I'd felt most of my Christian life: entangled, weighed down under a heavy yoke, in bondage, in debt, and, most of all, as if I were estranged from Christ. It also showed me *why* I felt that way; my obsession with goodness had nullified Christ's work in my life. Because I hadn't gone his way, I was on my own.

But he eventually got to me. He showed me that I sat in a jail cell with an open door but kept putting the chains back on myself instead of running free. He walked alongside me as I discovered the futility of trying to be good by myself, and he offered to rescue me, showing me what measure of grace he had already given me at the cross and at the moment I believed. But his way, as he revealed to me in Galatians, was nothing like my way. I could go my way and be forever frustrated at my never-ending debt, or I could accept his way of grace and faith and Spirit.

In time I realized that he loved me, not because of what I did but because of what he did through Christ on the cross. I finally ran wildly to his grace-filled arms, done with my chains. What had always felt like duty and obligation now felt like crazy freedom.

Grace for Every Day

As I shut the dresser drawer, finished with laundry for a few blessed days, I remembered what that freedom felt like. I remembered the feeling of my heart coming alive to his love, and how I had greedily received it and had wanted to give it away so generously.

The gospel regarding my salvation had been so clear.

But something had happened along the way.

The goodness gospel had silently and covertly wormed its way in again, bringing confusion, tripping me up. I found myself, once again, in Galatians, and it shone a light into the state of my heart: "Are you so foolish? Having begun in the Spirit, are you now being made perfect by the flesh?" (Gal. 3:3).

My goodness obsession was flaring up again, evidenced by my concerns about being good enough for God or for other people. I recognized that I'd understood what the gospel meant for salvation, but clearly I was still grasping what it meant for my everyday life. I realized that if I was not diligent and on guard, my goodness obsession would continue morphing and infecting new and different areas of my life. I thought about how it had affected me in ministry, how I'd wrestled with what it meant to be a good pastor's wife, and how I'd had to put my goodness obsession to death in that area by learning to rely on the Holy Spirit's power. I thought about how having our first child had sent me into a tailspin of comparison and feelings of failure and how I'd had to continually brawl with my obsession, pinning my need to control down to the ground. And I thought about my writing and how I'd grappled with the wickedest of feelings and motivations and how I'd had to learn to write by faith rather than for my own glory or by my own skill.

There, in my boys' bedroom, I prayed.

God, help me see how your gospel is meant to saturate my life. Show me what you want from me in my everyday life.

He immediately reminded me of 2 Corinthians 12:9: "My strength is made perfect in weakness." I suppose he knows, then, that I am weak and isn't expecting me to be strong. I suppose, then, I cannot manage my life. Considering my mothering, I suppose I cannot control or change my children, and I cannot work hard enough to produce men of valor. *I am weak. I have no authority to change the hearts of my children.*

But he didn't stop there. He reminded me of Paul's words in the next verse: "For when I am weak, then I am strong" (2 Cor. 12:10).

This is so what I want: to know deep in my soul that a good mother is not one who bakes intricate treats, who schools a certain way, who manages her household within an inch of its life, or who has her children in a million wonderful activities. A good mother is one who acknowledges her need for the power of God to train and teach and change the hearts of her children.

This is also what I want to know about being a wife, church member, community volunteer, and every other role I play—that the most important thing I can do each day is *not* to be good or rely on myself but to trust God and acknowledge my weakness. He will take my meager offering and turn it into a miracle. This is what I need to know down deep in my soul: how Christ's gospel of grace is for every single day.

And isn't this what we all need to know? Don't we all need to be free from the rubbish of our goodness obsession, to stop thinking of ourselves and discover what God wants from us? Don't we all need to know what it means to wake up every day and walk by faith, live in grace, and walk in the Spirit rather than stubbornly or ignorantly reverting back to external rituals, striving, and self-sufficiency? Don't we all need to awaken to the reality of the new creation God is making us deep in the unseen places? Don't we all need to allow him to take us to his heart and remove once and for all the chains we continue to put on ourselves?

Perhaps that's it exactly: we not only need to know what God wants *from* us, we also need to know what he wants *for* us.

2

The Most Important Things

A S A CHURCH-PLANTING PASTOR'S WIFE, I know hospitality comes with the territory. In fact, we started our church in our home, so I have learned how to stuff people in every last crevice of my living room and I have more chairs in my house than the average woman has decorative pillows on her bed. I can whip up Texas sheet cake without a recipe, I know what people will likely bring to a potluck (dessert) and what they likely won't (a main dish), and I keep an ever-replenished stash of coffee and every sugar substitute known to man in my pantry. And I buy toilet paper in bulk.

Although I've grown accustomed to fingerprints on the walls and stains in the carpet from the flow of people through our home, it took me many years to come to terms with the inevitable chaos and messes that accompany hospitality. I used to be scared of having people in my home, primarily because I was scared of doing it wrong.

As a result of my fear, my first attempts at hospitality were focused on controlling every last detail. I spent an inordinate amount of time planning menus and preparing large, intricate meals. I cleaned the house from top to bottom and lit candles reserved solely for such occasions. Just before our guests arrived, I would rush through the house, yelling at my children for touching the couch pillows that I had just karate-chopped in an attempt to achieve the perfect middle creases. Then the doorbell would ring and I'd greet our guests with as calm a smile as I could muster.

I fretted over so much: Was the food good? Did the glasses come out of the dishwasher with that weird film again, and did our guests notice? Was it too hot or too cold in the house? Was the conversation good? Did they think my husband and I told funny stories and were enjoyable to be with? Were the kids well-behaved?

I fretted and fussed over every last detail, so much so that by the time dinner was done, I was done too. I was worn out by it all and silently willing our guests to leave—but to leave, of course, with a favorable impression of me, my home, and my family. I thought so much about myself and about creating the perfect atmosphere that I probably appeared only halfheartedly interested in our guests.

I missed the point of hospitality entirely.

Emphasizing details and tasks and things rather than love and relationships, I attempted to serve people with a picture of perfection, but without loving them. I dictated to them how they should be honored—coordinated dishes and placemats, charming conversation, and delicious homemade meals, of course—rather than simply honoring them by being fully present and in relationship with them. Instead of thinking of how I might express honor to guests, I concentrated on tasks and things and my own honor.

I have a tendency to do this in so many areas of my life, but most often and most debilitating in how I relate with and respond to God. In my attempt to make an impact in God's name and be a "good" Christian, I serve him in a variety of ways. I line ministry opportunities up like my karate-chopped pillows and plow through them one by one, looking up every once in a while to see if God is watching and if he's pleased, inevitably getting irritated at people with needs that interrupt my agenda. Through my good works and activities and service, I dictate to Jesus how he should be honored. Working myself up into a frantic, over-scheduled mess, I just grow burdened and weary and do not love anyone or anything.

When I do this, I miss the point of the gospel entirely and, inadvertently, make the Christian life all about me and my own abilities and efforts and practices. I make a beeline for activity and works, hoping that my goodness will help me receive the joy and peace I want from the Lord. The externals associated with my faith—any activity that proves my devotion to God—take priority over internal transformation. My attempts to order my life and squeeze spiritual growth from pure effort—to be good in honor of God but apart from God—reveal only pride and self-sufficiency and do nothing to lead me to the joy and abundant life Jesus promises. So I get burdened, weary, and cynical: Is this all there is to Jesus and his gospel?

But just as hospitality without love is not hospitality at all, external effort to produce heart change in myself and others is not the gospel. It's the goodness gospel, but it's not Christ's gospel.

Whether we realize it or not, we're hearing the goodness gospel all the time, so it's hard to know and remember the most important things and to think about how the gospel of Jesus applies to our everyday lives. In the last exercise class I attended, for example, the teacher closed with several stretches and calming clichés that too closely resemble what we say to each other in Bible study: "Be the change you want." We say it in more Christian terms of course—"Just read your Bible and pray more"—but it's the same message: that our spiritual growth, our goodness, and our kingdom impact are up to us. We give it more focus, more willpower, more discipline, but are we focused on the most important things? We're too busy lining up our good works for efficient karate chops to think about the *why* of what we're doing. And we're too frenzied by conjuring up our own motivations for those works to simply let the true gospel settle in us and then rise up to do its work through us.

Questioning God

The truth is that we're often asking the right question: What does God want from us? But we're asking it of the wrong audience. We're asking anyone and everyone *but* God.

The right question asked of the wrong audience is what happens when we are obsessed with goodness and our religious reputation rather than being intently obsessed with God and his gospel. We want to know what God wants from us, but we ask other people, we read what other "good" people are doing, and we imitate what they're doing, because it's easier that way. We can make a list of what they say, check their suggestions off one by one, and evaluate ourselves by the list. So we pick someone out whom we admire, or we join a church full of people doing things a certain way, or we read books about spiritual practices, and we follow all their suggestions. If they appear to be people who follow God and they make definitive statements about spiritual practices, we'll, of course, immediately follow their lead. Because we love God and we genuinely want to please him. And this is the way, right? But then we feel a little funny and evaluated when we're not doing what everyone else says we should be doing. And we feel a little funny and judgmental when others around us aren't doing what we're doing, and we start to disassociate from them.

But what is happening in our hearts? What is happening in the hearts of others? Can these external representations of religious practice—of goodness—give us any true indication? This is why it's dangerous to ask the right question of the wrong audience, because typically other people will answer with externals: you should go to this type of church (or not), you should read these types of books (or not), you should go on a Christian dating website (or not), you should avoid alcohol (or not), you should sell your fancy car and give away the proceeds (or not). The list could go on infinitely, and one could argue that all of these external practices have value. But are these the things God wants from us? Are these the most important things? Are these the things most closely tied to the gospel?

I mentioned that I'm a pastor's wife, and not just a pastor's wife but a church-planting pastor's wife. Who let her husband start a church in her living room. Who has people over for dinner. Who plans a menu ahead of time. Who karate-chops pillows. Perhaps you got stuck on that part because you're not a person who has people in your home and you started imagining a meal far greater than anything I actually make, and you started feeling pretty unspiritual in comparison, which led to you beating yourself up or immediately making a list of people whom you should invite over.

Or you're on the other extreme, and you've already figured you're going to stop reading because you don't want to hear a list of things you should be doing from another goody-two-shoes pastor's wife.

But this is my point exactly. We are way too concerned with what other people are doing and trying to match or judge what they are doing. We are jumping ahead to a great question (What does God want from me?) but asking it of the wrong audience (other people) and skipping the gospel question entirely.

The most important and life-giving thing we can do as followers of Christ is to consider what God wants for us as presented in the gospel and to ask the right questions of the right Person.

It seems to me that we don't even take our questions to him. We have our way of goodness that we think pleases God, a way driven by our flesh, by the opinions of others, by effort, and by worldly wisdom. And we just kind of flail around in it, looking for joy in futility.

But it's pretty clear that God has another way entirely and it's through the gospel of grace that Jesus talked about and lived and continues to pour out. His way—the way to true life—is through death. He died and rose again so that we could die and rise to real life in him. And *that's exactly* why we find his way so difficult, and turn instead to a list of external regulations. His free grace is received only when we give ourselves up to death, including the death of trying to be good on our own.

We too often stand just outside his way, thinking we're knocking down the barriers to the abundant life with our good Christian behaviors and activities and choices, and wondering if this is all there is to the power and grace of God. God, however, offers his answer—the right answer—to the right question. If we will just listen and go his way, he will move us from our good-striving to the grace we desperately crave to live in.

Don't you get tired sometimes? Don't you crave freedom from activity for the sake of activity, freedom from trying to maintain a good-girl image, and freedom from trying to figure out a way to get God's love?

The answer is not to do more. The answer is to simply take our questions to him.

God, what do you want for *us?*

God, what do you want from *us?*

He will point to the gospel, not just the gospel for our salvation but the gospel for our everyday lives.

Because the gospel applied to the everyday will change us.

The gospel quiets the clamor and comparisons, the swirling online world, and the self-accusations. The gospel tells us to rest because Christ is enough, but it also leads us to respond in obedience when God asks things of us that are counter to what others and our own hearts tell us are important. The gospel shows us how to receive from God what we need in order to truly live and what we need to serve others with joy, sacrificial love, and power. So we *must* know the gospel for every day. We must allow him to break our obsession with goodness, and our obsession with goodness can only be broken by the gospel of Christ.

Old Realities

When I realized that I barely knew how the gospel applied to my life after my salvation, I went digging around in Scripture, trying to figure it all out. I discovered that the true gospel is not about goodness and that nowhere in the Bible does Jesus say, "Be good." He never said anything that should lead us to think we're capable on our own of being good or doing good. In fact, he had a few choice words for all those who thought they were good apart from him.

The gospel is actually about wickedness and how that wickedness didn't just become goodness but became righteousness, a forever right-with-God-ness for those who believe. The gospel is that Jesus took the punishment for all our wickedness, completed every possible to-do list of goodness for us *so that we don't have to*, and that he *chose* to·do all these things because he *wanted* to. The gospel is that we are free from trying to be good, because we actually can't be; Christ became our sin so that we could become not just good but the very righteousness of God.[1]

First of all, it's insanely crazy awesome that God would rescue me from my sin like that. And even though it's insanely crazy awesome, I can somewhat fathom a point of rescue, like a slate being wiped clean. But what I struggle to fathom is that this same rescue continues throughout my life in Christ, that his mercies are new for me every day, and that he is responsible for my spiritual growth (or what some seminary types call *sanctification*).

What I also discovered is that our attempts at goodness are actually residue from our old reality, the reality of who we were and how we lived *before* we knew Christ. Our old reality is that we were dead—lifeless, cold, completely unable to know and serve and experience God, and enslaved to our fleshly desires. Paul describes a people still living in their old reality:

> You should no longer walk as the rest of the Gentiles walk, in the futility of their mind, having their understanding darkened, being alienated from the life of God, because of the ignorance that is in them, because of the blindness of their heart; who, being past feeling, have given themselves over to lewdness, to work all uncleanness with greediness. (Eph. 4:17–19)

All of us have lived in this old reality, as alienated enemies of God, as hard-hearted, unrepentant sinners. In this state of deadness, God offers his rescue through Christ. Some reject God's rescue outright. But there are others in this state of deadness who respond to God's overtures of grace by pointing proudly to their "goodness," their so-called self-righteousness, although it is not really righteousness at all compared to the righteousness of God.

Self-sufficiency tends to feel so right and good to us, but it is really a path of grave danger. According to Paul, a certain portion of God's wrath is reserved for those who outright reject him.[2] But there is another portion that hits closer to our religious home: God's wrath is also reserved for the self-righteous—those who appear to love God based on their external activities but whose hearts are far from him, those who are working to create their own righteousness apart from the pursuing love of Christ.[3] These are the religious people who claim to love God and are obsessed with being good, but who "despise the riches of His goodness, forbearance, and longsuffering, not knowing that the goodness of God leads you to repentance"

(Rom 2·4) They look proudly to their own goodness rather than to the goodness of God. These too invite God's wrath because self-righteousness is not the way he's mapped out for us to be in right relationship with him. In other words, he doesn't expect us to be good enough for him. He knows that we cannot be.

We know quite by logic that our rejection of God leads us away from him and, in turn, invites his wrath. But do we know deep down in our hearts that our attempts at being good Christians or good wives or good mothers or good employers or whatever it is that we're attempting to be good at through our own efforts are not his way and are just as dead—and just as deadly?

A shudder went through me when I read about myself in Romans 2. In reality, it read me, running an X-ray machine over my heart and revealing my stubborn self-sufficiency and how disgusting and dishonoring it is to the God who has already made me sufficient. All that effort, all my attempts at goodness to impress God, and none of it moved him. The X-ray also revealed the most important things, bringing the answers to my questions into clear view.

A Glorious Mystery and a New Reality

Having laid aside the goodness gospel, here we are with our questions, turning them over in our minds, trying to determine what God wants both for us and from us. Do you also see the answers becoming clear?

Because his grace is a gift he imparts in our hearts, his eyes are there as well. He is sifting through our outward appearance, our activities, our reputation, and whatever outward image we've created for ourselves, and zeroing in on our hearts. This is the first and most important thing he wants from us—our hearts in full surrender to his way rather than our futile ways. And this is his way: he wants us to give ourselves to him through faith in Jesus's death and resurrection. He wants us to give ourselves to him every day.

His way is to look at our hearts: Is the heart changed? Or as Paul so often puts it: Is the heart circumcised?

This immediately highlights the inadequacies of goodness in pleasing God, because we cannot change our hearts. We falsely believe that a certain ordering of behaviors or religious practices can reach down deep into this mystery and cause some type of transformation, but they can't.

Only One has access to the heart. Only One can see it, know it fully, and change it. Like the valves that control the flow of blood to and from the physical heart, we can open or close his access, but he is the only one who can enter and, by his Spirit, overhaul everything inside.

God's way to true life and godliness is a glorious mystery because it happens in the invisible place of our hearts. Through faith in Christ, we are ushered into an unseen and intangible new reality, what Oswald Chambers calls the reality of redemption.[4] Our dead, cold spiritual hearts start beating. The circumcision of the heart, that Holy Spirit mark made in the unseen places, grants us access to God himself and opens to us the treasury of the immeasurable riches of Christ.

God himself.

The immeasurable riches of Christ.

These are what God wants *for* us—for our hearts to come alive by the Spirit's power and for this new reality to be what we walk in, move in, belong in, and enjoy God in. That we live our every day in.

This new reality also automatically and passionately answers the question, "What does God want from us?" Instead of a rote religious checklist of goodness, we gladly offer everything we can give. It is this new reality that empowers and motivates all our outward expressions of faith, making them all—every single one— expressions of response and worship.

We did nothing to get into this new reality except receive by faith all that God graciously offered us in Christ. In identifying with

Christ we submitted ourselves to self-death, and then God made us alive to himself with the same power that made Christ alive again.

And so he wants our hearts from us; he wants us fully in by faith. And then he wants another thing from us—to receive what Christ has won for us.

Receive is a key word in our new reality, because God pours an avalanche of gifts and grace and mercy upon us in Christ. We could spend a lifetime looking into these things, and we will, but we can start with these gifts:

> God made us alive, and he did this even when we were still his enemies, because he loves us and is rich in mercy (Eph. 2:4).
>
> We are no longer enslaved to sin (Rom. 6:11).
>
> He has wiped away our sins and the list of requirements from the law that we couldn't fulfill on our own (Col. 2:14).
>
> He has given us the Spirit as a seal, a help, and a guarantee for our future redemption (John 16:7; Rom. 8:26; 2 Cor. 5:5).
>
> We are complete in him. Nothing else is needed to be right with God (Col. 2:10).
>
> We escape all condemnation (Rom. 8:1).
>
> We become sons and daughters of God and, therefore, brothers and sisters with Christ. We are co-heirs with him (vv. 14, 17).
>
> God is for us (v. 31).
>
> We can never again be separated from God and his love (vv. 38–39).
>
> We have life and peace (v. 6).

As I discovered these truths, it was quite powerful for me to change the pronouns from "we" to "I" and from "us" to "me." Because of what Christ did, *I* have been made alive to enjoy God. *I* am free from the power of sin and death. *I* have the Holy Spirit dwelling in *me*, and he leads me, helps me, crucifies my flesh, convicts me, prays for me, and helps me know the mind of God. *I* am a daughter of God. God is for *me*.

These are the glorious and immeasurable riches found in Christ, and I achieved none of them by being good. I received them. You received them. And—this is key to crushing our goodness obsession—just as we were ushered into our new reality by faith, we are to *continue* living by faith. This is where, unfortunately, we get tripped up, and we will address this struggle in the next chapter. But for now, let us see that because God works in the internal, in the unseen places only he can go, we have a clear indication of what it will mean to *remain* in this new reality, to stand firm, to walk by faith, to live in grace, and to walk in the Spirit. Our focus must remain on what God thinks are the most important things, and none of those are rote external practices.

The way God answers our questions changes everything, doesn't it? Because it means that the one thing he wants for us is to receive from him and let what he gives well up and overflow from the inside out in response.

This has everything to do with salvation, but it also has everything to do with the everyday. Once we discover how the gospel applies to our everyday, the goodness addiction is broken in our lives. We, instead, become addicts of grace, faith, and joy. We no longer hide our weaknesses because we recognize that our weaknesses are opportunities to trumpet the grace of God.

We recognize the call to come and die with Christ is also the call to come and live.

Receive and Respond

Jesus showed this laser-like focus on internal matters and receiving from him when he interacted with Mary and Martha in Martha's home. We typically consider the story of Mary and Martha to be a statement on having a devotional life, which is a good and necessary application from the story, but I think, even more, it illustrates the answer to our question of what God wants from us.

Martha always gets the bad rap in this story, and I feel a little protective of her since I'm more of the get-things-done kind of person than the sit-and-let-someone-else-take-care-of-it kind of person. In the glare of Mary's halo, we often are blinded to the fact that Martha did right and good things. She willingly invited Jesus into her home, and although they temporarily fall out of view in the focus of the story, a hungry (and presumably messy) crowd was tagging along behind him. Warm hospitality was culturally expected and highly valued, therefore Martha's rushing around karate-chopping pillows and setting out food—the fact that she was serving—wasn't what Jesus addressed when she went to him to whine about Mary's passivity. He addressed her anxiousness, her distracted heart. She was, he said, missing the most important thing, the thing that Mary got right.

What did Mary get right? Mary, in fact, had plopped down among the men at the feet of Jesus, what would have been considered a bold, countercultural statement. She positioned herself in a way that said clearly, "I am a disciple of Jesus. I want to be where he is."

Martha loved Jesus and wanted to do good things for him. But she erred when she dictated to him how he would best be honored and served, which was essentially that he should be honored by her goodness.

Mary immediately recognized the most important thing, the one thing Jesus wanted from her: to receive from him. She put herself in a position to listen to him, learn from him, and submit to him, and Jesus commended her for it.

God wants the same thing from us. He simply wants us to follow him, receive from him, submit to him, and, as we will discover later, let what we receive from him compel us outward to serve and love people. Just as Jesus likely would have said to Mary, "Arise and go," he says to us, "As you go, make disciples."

Receive and respond. But we can't respond until we've received from him.

These are the most important things.

This is what God wants from us.

Does this cause a welling-up in your heart of joy and freedom like it does in mine? *Why,* I asked myself, *would anyone ever, having experienced this new reality—a reality of redemption—turn around and go back to her old ways of being goodness-obsessed?*

But I had.

I needed to know and understand: *Why did I go back?*

3

You Can't Go Back Again

I'M *NOT SWEET. I should be, but I'm not.* That's what I thought to myself as I pulled into the garage and closed it behind me, safe from the opinions of others in the cocoon of my home. I'd been thinking of someone who *is* sweet and how much I loved her, and how I wished I were sweet like her. And although I was ensconced in the comfort of home, the familiar bombardment began and I couldn't find a way to hide from all the thoughts—all the thoughts of everything I'm not.

This season has been a weird one, and I've been and felt weird because of it. I've come face-to-face with my faults and weaknesses and mess-ups. The spotlight has shone brightly on everything I'm not, and I've struggled to turn it back to God and who he has made me and what he's given me to do. As a result, I've shrunk back and questioned just about everything about myself.

I've shrunk back in relationships, worrying too much about what others think of me and always assuming they think the worst.

I've shrunk back in ministry, unsure of my gifts, unsure of my place, and feeling as if I was on the outside, mostly because I put myself there and kept myself there.

I've shrunk back as a mother, letting my failures and insecurities lead.

I've shrunk back in my writing, afraid to remove the protection I've placed around my heart, uncertain that I have anything to say and, above all, questioning if this is God's idea or if it's been my selfish idea all along.

I've even shrunk back a little from God, holding parts of myself away from him.

The tape recording of everything I'm not has played in my head for a few months now, and I knew it was happening but I couldn't put words to it, and I certainly haven't known how to make it stop.

It's all been fear. Fear of failure. Fear of not having anything of value to give. Fear of being different or disliked. Fear of writing what I don't really know or live. Fear of missing it. Fear of being disconnected or lonely. You name it, I've probably feared it.

But in the midst of this season I had another thought invade: *What if I lived as if the gospel were true every hour of every day? How would that change things?*

That's how I recognized it's all been fear, because I suddenly saw my thoughts and my life in light of the freedom and the power of the gospel, and realized how much I wasn't living in freedom and power. Instead, I've been chained, paralyzed, stuck, and completely stopped in my tracks. All by fear.

So I went to God and laid it all out on the table, weary and desperate, because fear makes you weary and desperate. I told him how I was weary of writing because of the pressure, through fear, I was placing on myself. I told him how I was so sick of thinking through the filter of the opinions of others, and I confessed this idolatry. I told him how I hadn't gone all out in relationships because I was so intently focused on my own inadequacies and so fearful that I wouldn't be loved. I told him how I hadn't used my gifts fully because I'd compared my gifts with others' and had come up short every time.

God, please speak to me. I am desperate for you. That's all I could say. It's all I wanted.

And he did, taking me directly to Psalm 27:1.

> The LORD is my light and my salvation;
>> Whom shall I fear?
>> The LORD is the strength of my life;
>> Of whom shall I be afraid?

I sighed.

How many times do I go through periods like this of fear or doubt or sin because I've returned to my frenemy, the goodness gospel, without even realizing it? When I don't think about what I'm thinking about, my natural tendency is to try to please people and earn approval and be a good little girl, because that's what I'm supposed to be.

But if I lived as if the gospel were true for me every hour of every day, there would never be room for fear or any of the rest of it. If I believed God and his Word, I wouldn't revert to my own efforts to please him or anyone else. But I hadn't been living free from fear, and God made that clear to me in the gentle yet firm way he does when he convicts.

In that moment, my heart soared. I chose to release my fears one by one. I chose to turn my mind from everything I'm not to everything I am *because of God.* I chose to look at my roles, responsibilities, and opportunities through the eyes of faith and to trust him as I pursued those. I chose to believe I had absolutely no reason to fear, especially other people and their opinions of me.

The next morning I had to rechoose all those things, because the thoughts are habitual. But I'm finding already that the more I think about the gospel and Christ's message of love, approval, and purpose, the more I am intentional with everything I actually am and free of the fears that come with everything I'm not.

I think most of us do this without even realizing it, not thinking about what we're thinking about, not considering whether it's biblical truth or not. Our thoughts lead us around on a leash, and we feel powerless to stop them.

That's why we go back to the goodness gospel—because our thoughts lead us there every time. In *Christless Christianity*, Michael Horton says,

> Because the gospel is so odd, even to us Christians, that we have to get it again and again. The law is innate and intuitive, while the gospel is an external announcement. Our default setting is law rather than gospel, imperatives (things to do or feel) rather than indicatives (things to believe). Everyone assumes the law. It is the gospel that is a surprising announcement none of us had a right to expect. As such, it has to be told—again and again.[1]

As such, we must hear it believing, read it believing, and tell it to ourselves believing again and again and again.

Gospel Illiteracy

We go back because living by our goodness is innate and it's also, I believe, because we're gospel illiterate. Our confusion develops because we know the gospel but we don't know how to *apply* the gospel. We know what the gospel means for salvation, but we have no idea what it means for every day. We don't know what it means for how we live and serve, so we serve to be good rather than out of response to the gospel. We don't know that it informs our Bible reading, prayer, and other spiritual disciplines, so we practice them dutifully instead of with joy. We so easily lose sight of what the most important things are. We simply don't know what it is that God offers us, what he wants for us, and what he wants from us.

This gospel illiteracy shows itself in many ways. Rose Marie Miller, in describing her own gospel illiteracy, gives one example.

> The gospel was not my working theology: Mine was moralism and legalism—a religion of duty and self control through human willpower. The goal was self-justification, not the justification by faith in Christ that the gospel offers. But, as many people can tell you, moralism and legalism can "pass" for Christianity, at least outwardly, in the good times. It is only when crises come that you find there is no foundation on which to stand. And crises are what God used to reveal my heart's true need for him.[2]

Goodness obsession shows itself in a variety of ways and affects different people in different ways. I see it in the eyes and hear it in the words of the women in my life, women who genuinely love the Lord, want to honor him, and want to make an impact on others in the name of Jesus. They know grace and they know God, yet they struggle to walk in what they know or sometimes even to discern how the gospel applies to situations they're facing.

My friend Marylyn and I talk about this when we get together for coffee. She tells me how she's trying to do singleness well and not believe terrible lies about God, like the enemy's whispering that God withholds good gifts from his kids or that he's somehow forgotten her. The worst and hardest one to fight, she says, is the lie that if she were good at being single and trusting God well enough, her goodness would magically unlock the gift from God she most wants. The lie is both that her goodness and what she can get are the goal. Marylyn fights hard to trust God and she serves him well, and I think she honors him with her singleness, and we talk all the time about how to break our goodness addiction by clinging to the grace of Christ.

I have another sweet friend who talks to me about how she leaves church feeling worse than when she arrived because when she listens to sermons, she hears a to-do list. The pastor speaks about how God's love compels her to serve, but my friend hears that she should try harder and do more. She's struggling to relate to the Person of God in an intimate way, to know his love, and to walk in the freedom of that relationship.

I have several friends who, for a season, were heavily influenced by church leaders entangled in goodness obsessions themselves. My friends were subtly taught they could lose their salvation if they weren't holy enough or didn't perform well enough in their evangelistic efforts. They became insulated in a like-minded group and were influenced to question other ministries their leaders deemed too lax with holiness and too loose with grace. I witnessed their resulting struggle to come out from under legalism and to discern what the gospel really is, how to live by the Spirit rather than by the law, and how to keep from swinging to the opposite extreme of grace without responsibility.

The goodness gospel is all around us, showing itself in a variety of ways. *Do more. Try harder. Discipline yourself. Change your habits. Be a better Christian. Just go to church more. Work hard to be a good wife and a good mom. Obey so you can get something. You just don't have enough faith. God might be mad at you. Strive with good works to erase the shame and guilt.*

I get to talk to women who are struggling with grace and freedom all the time. Some, feeling like complete failures, think they cannot receive God's forgiveness unless they perform some kind of penance. Some cannot understand the perspectives of other women because they are so sure of the rightness of their own. Some feel isolated and alone but won't let people in because they are so afraid of the possibility of others seeing their weaknesses.

Some are working to achieve standards for themselves that God has not put on them. Some cannot comprehend how God could be loving and gracious rather than angry and disengaged. Some are working earnestly to please God and to earn the approval of a man, their parents, or other women.

Their symptoms are different, but they all have a goodness addiction like me.

I used to think that God brought specific women along for me to know that were addicted to goodness and confused by grace because it was my story too, and I could share my story with them. But then I realized that this is the story of most women, that it's a spiritual epidemic plaguing our churches because it plagues our hearts. We're born with a fleshly pull toward pride and/or self-condemnation, and, even though we are genuine followers of Christ, our religious practices and misunderstandings and misapplications of the gospel often only feed all the wrong things in us. We all need the Holy Spirit to transform our hearts and help us walk in freedom. We all need to move from good to grace.

We revert to the goodness gospel not only because it's an innate pull fed by gospel illiteracy but also because it has an appearance of wisdom.

> Therefore, if you died with Christ from the basic principles of the world, why, as though living in the world, do you subject yourselves to regulations—"Do not touch, do not taste, do not handle,". . . according to the commandments and doctrines of men? *These things indeed have an appearance of wisdom in self-imposed religion, false humility, and neglect of the body, but are of no value against the indulgence of the flesh.* (Col. 2:20–23, emphasis added)

The goodness gospel is typically couched in spiritual terms and is difficult to differentiate from the true gospel because it draws our attention to external practices, and often "good" external practices at that. The goodness gospel comes wrapped in words that make you feel more spiritual if you practice them.

The Galatian churches were caught up in all these things. Converted Jews were telling converted Gentiles that Christ was not enough, that they should also become circumcised in order to be true believers. Paul, however, was firm with them, even rebuking Peter when he huddled with the Jewish faction, separating and therefore condemning the uncircumcised faction. "Know this," he said. "This persuasion does not come from him who calls you" (Gal. 5:8). In other words, this goodness gospel is not the gospel of Christ.

We can't just get grace once. We must receive grace every day and soak every area of our lives in it. That can only happen by becoming gospel literate, by saturating ourselves in Scripture. Becoming gospel literate helps us to discern when the goodness gospel is speaking, so we can remain in our true reality of redemption.

Knowing that we all have this fleshly tendency, we must learn to recognize and be on guard against returning to goodness after we've received grace. Based upon what we see in the New Testament, it doesn't appear to be all that unusual for believers to return to their old reality, to return to some form of self-justification. If the Galatians, before whose eyes and for whose sakes Jesus Christ was clearly portrayed as crucified, turned so quickly again to the goodness gospel, we must not beat ourselves up over our struggles to understand and apply the true gospel.[3]

However, we must also not resign ourselves to never understanding or applying the true gospel. It may not be unusual to revert to the goodness gospel, but it's a serious and consequential mistake for many reasons. Reverting to a goodness gospel removes Christ from the equation entirely and creates a system where we have a debt that, no matter what we do or accomplish or perfect, we can never fully pay. It guarantees we cannot please God.

ID Cards

When I think about living by the goodness gospel as compared to the true gospel, I think of ID cards.

During the summer before my senior year of high school, word got out that the administration planned to make us all wear our school ID cards around our necks on lanyards the following year. I suppose they were worried that random people might try to sneak into high school and learn something, so they needed a clear indication that each student actually belonged on campus.

As a teenage girl who cared enough about her appearance to carry around a gigantic aerosol can of hairspray in her purse each day (to spruce up my gravity-defying bangs, of course), I was devastated. My girlfriends and I considered together every possible outfit scenario and how this edict might affect our wardrobe choices.

Somehow I made it through that year with my bangs and my pride safely in place. However, the minute I graduated, I happily flung that lanyard off and never looked at it again. I was more than glad to graduate into the college world where my ID card actually meant something: it allowed me access to everything from dorms to meals, football games, and movie discounts, and, best of all, I didn't have to wear it around my neck.

While my college ID meant everything, my high school ID meant absolutely nothing anymore, other than capturing my gravity-defying bangs for posterity. Otherwise, it had no power to access anything. If I swiped my high school card at the college cafeteria, it couldn't access my meal plan. If I tried to use it to reserve football tickets, I'd get it handed right back to me. My high school ID only represented an old reality; I had a new one that offered me access to everything I needed and wanted as a college student. It would've been pure foolishness to rely on my old ID.

It's just as foolish for us to return to living in our old reality before Christ. We've been delivered from the power of darkness and conveyed into the kingdom of the Son of God's love, we have access to God and everything we need for life and godliness, and we have the power of God that raised Christ from the dead coursing through our veins.[4] Why would we go back to death, defeat, and self-sufficiency? Paul agrees that it's pure foolishness, this starting by faith and through the Spirit's power and then returning to self-sufficient works:

> O foolish Galatians! Who has bewitched you that you should not obey the truth, before whose eyes Jesus Christ was clearly portrayed among you as crucified? This only I want to learn from you: Did you receive the Spirit by the works of the law, or by the hearing of faith? Are you so foolish? Having begun in the Spirit, are you now being made perfect by the flesh? (Gal. 3:1–3)

Discern and Recognize

How can we learn to discern and recognize those things that lead us to live from our old reality rather than our new?

The first thing we must know about returning to the goodness gospel is that it is often cyclical and a type of bondage.

In my service to the church, I think to myself much too often, *I'm not doing enough.* The needs and opportunities in our church are many and varied, so much so that I can get overwhelmed and confused with how best to give my time and energy outside the home. But it's not just the number of needs and opportunities available and it's not that I'm looking for more to add to my plate. It's that I so easily revert to performance in regard to this role. If my calendar is full, if I am having people in our home for meals, if I'm serving in tangible and measurable ways, I feel pretty good about the way I'm filling the role I've inherited by way of my husband. But when I am unable to meet with someone, I disappoint someone, or my service to do list is thin, that nagging feeling rises to the surface: *I'm not doing enough.*

So what do I do? If I am living according to the goodness gospel, my feelings of weakness don't lead me to fall on the grace of God. Instead, they lead me to work harder: make lists, add things to my calendar, smile bigger, impress people, do lots of stuff, and do it all well. So then what happens? I'm human, so I fail at attaining my standards of perfection. And then what? I feel weak, powerless, and hopeless that I will ever be able to serve God how I think I should be serving him. The cycle of try-harder, do-better begins again.

However, there is another way of responding to these thoughts, a way that breaks the cyclical bondage of the goodness gospel. I can respond according to the gospel of grace, but it requires that I'm alert to what I'm thinking and being compelled toward. Thoughts based on the goodness gospel will always compel me to strive and produce an uncertainty of God's love unless I am striving. The gospel, however, leads me to consider the heart behind the thought that I'm not doing enough and take it in prayer to God. I ask him, "Is this condemnation or Spirit-led conviction?" By consistently responding in this manner, I've discovered that Spirit-led conviction is specific and, even when difficult, is hopeful. Condemnation is couched in general terms (*you're not doing enough*) and leaves me feeling hopeless. Instead of succumbing to try-harder, do-better, I am compelled to ask the Lord, "Am I being faithful with what you've given me to do?" and wait for and obey his lead.

Do *you* recognize your goodness addiction and how it shows itself in your life?

Do you often feel separated from God? Do you often find yourself thinking, *I'm not a good enough Christian*? Do you criticize yourself and others? Do you often find yourself wanting to be known and recognized for your good works? Do you find yourself serving without any inner motivation to serve? Do you find yourself doing things to look good to other people? Do you often feel guilty? Do you feel like you have never experienced a life of freedom and joy? Are you quick to understand God's rules and judgment but slow to understand his love? Do you often seek after the approval of those around you? Do you often question whether or not you have the Lord's approval? These are signs that the goodness gospel is front and center in your life. And it feels like bondage, doesn't it?

Salvation but Not Sanctification?

The second thing we must know about the goodness gospel is it says the gospel is for salvation but not for sanctification.

We think of the gospel as sufficient for salvation, and we continually look back to it and say, "Whew, I'm forgiven," and we look forward to heaven and feel hopeful—but we lack any real sense of what the gospel means for our present. The goodness gospel has us starting by faith then trying really hard to grow by our own efforts, and there is, if we're honest, no joy in it at all.

In actuality, the gospel is for our present just as much as it is for our past and our future. The gospel is that through faith in Christ, he makes us alive to a whole new reality. This is a reality we are invited to dwell in, walk in, and most importantly, enjoy God in. God has not only ushered us into this new reality through Christ but he has also given us everything we need to *continue* in this new reality and to grow in all spiritual wisdom and understanding.

God acts, pursues, transforms, grows, and does every other action that sanctifies us. We submit, repent, obey, and receive. He leads; we respond. We are not in the leadership position and God is not in the position of responsive evaluator. As he pursued us for salvation, he pursues us for sanctification and will do the work as we submit ourselves to his good leadership.

So one of the applications of the gospel for every day is that we don't have to convict or condemn ourselves. Often, when we read something in Scripture or hear an exhortation in a sermon, we think, *I need to work on that.* We convict ourselves and try to be better. We come up with a strategy to "fix" ourselves and be a better Christian. But did God convict us? There is a difference between us convicting ourselves and the Holy Spirit convicting us. One leads to guilt and condemnation and the other leads to godly sorrow, repentance, hope, and dependence.

Sanctification is led by the Spirit from start to finish. He does the convicting, forgiving, sanctifying, and transforming. "Now may the God of peace Himself sanctify you completely; and may your whole spirit, soul, and body be preserved blameless at the coming of our Lord Jesus Christ. He who calls you is faithful, who also will do it" (1 Thess. 5:23–24). We simply agree with his assessment, repent, and submit to and trust his leadership in changing us. There is peace and assurance in the Spirit.

The goodness gospel, on the other hand, says the gospel of grace is just for salvation, and that we must attain our spiritual growth after salvation or pay God back by doing good works.

As a teenager, at the height of my goodness obsession, I spent the obligatory ten minutes having a "quiet time" each school morning. During that time, I read devotional readings written for teenagers, which typically ended with application questions about my behavior. My favorite devotional readings involved lists, such as the fruits of the Spirit. I vividly remember taking the list, giving each fruit of the Spirit a day on my calendar, and committing to "working on" each one so I could get better at them. At the end of the time, I reasoned, I'd be a more joyful, patient, gentle person. And, even better, once I got through all the fruits, I could hit repeat, creating for myself an amazing trajectory of growth.

It's too bad I missed all the stuff that comes before that in the book of Galatians. You know, all that gospel, walk-in-the-Spirit stuff. And it's too bad that the message I received in the youth group at church was a medley of dos and don'ts that covered topics ranging from dancing to Halloween activities to exactly when and how and how long to have quiet times.

This was the message I received and was applying: you are saved by grace, but you are responsible for everything after that. Your growth, change, maturity, spiritual knowledge, even conviction—all of it is up to you. I suppose the idea I had of God was that he was pretty disengaged, except for when I did something wrong, and then he was eager to discipline me. I couldn't rely on him; I had to rely on myself. This idea created in me pride, self-condemnation, and a powerless and defeatist existence.

Everything we say we should be doing in the Christian life should be followed by, "And by the way, you can't do this. Only the Spirit of God can do this in you, so ask him to do it."

This is how the gospel is for every day.

And it is not what the goodness gospel tells us.

The Goodness Gospel Produces Pride

The hallmark of the goodness gospel is pride. We feel good about ourselves (and thus, we assume, God feels good about us) as long as we're doing well and completing the goodness checklist. By the way, that goodness checklist differs according to the circles we run in. If we're surrounded by academic types, we'll take pride in our knowledge and theology and apologetic abilities. If we're around those passionate about social justice, we'll take pride in how much we give away and how many we rescue or help.

Of course all of these things are good things, but they *can* be done from self-focus and pride and have nothing to do with God. As we walk in the goodness gospel, we will boast, at least to ourselves and quite possibly to others, about our choices, our knowledge, our convictions, our theology, and our good works. In other words, we boast in ourselves and our own abilities—in everything *but* the cross of Christ. And that is exactly how we can discern whether the goodness gospel or the true gospel is motivating us: the true gospel leads us to the cross and to an understanding that everything we've been given, even the very air we breathe, is a gift of grace. Most of all, the cross helps us understand that our salvation and our sanctification come through God's work on our behalf; therefore, every person has the opportunity to be reconciled to him by faith and no one can ever boast that they somehow played a part in it.

The Goodness Gospel Produces Self-Condemnation

If you walk in the goodness gospel for any length of time, you'll find that, at some point, the pendulum of pride always swings to the other extreme—self-condemnation. Being a false gospel based on human effort, it's only natural it would offer opportunity both for boasting and for feelings of failure and worthlessness.

Of course, when we're living under the goodness gospel, we are more concerned with external appearances and standards that we or others have set for ourselves than we are concerned with the reality of our sin. We focus on measurable standards.

But the rub, and there is always a rub with the goodness gospel, is when our effort produces no measurable results or when our perfectionistic plans fall through. What then? That challenges the very heart of the goodness gospel and shows us the futility of living according to human effort.

I recognized this in my own life through church planting. In 2008, our little family moved across the country to start a church. Prior to planting, my husband served in a large, established church. We were *very* comfortable in our life and ministry, and, I felt, successful leaders. But then we planted a church, and it was a huge struggle for the first few years. I suddenly saw our previous life with much more clarity. I had attributed my "success" in ministry to my own abilities and gifts but had likely never really known what it meant to walk by faith or depend on the Lord.

In that time, I began to recognize how walking in the goodness gospel led me to condemn myself based upon the lack of results we were seeing in our work. But the gospel, spoken through the Word of God, led me to something different. I saw with great clarity that the work of salvation and sanctification and spiritual fruit belong to God, and that I am simply a vessel he may choose to use. And so the struggle in church planting to get anything going was a severe mercy from God's hand for my benefit, because he taught me to depend on him, walk by faith, and trust him for any and all "results" we might (or might not) see.

The Goodness Gospel Produces Fear

One of the evidences of walking in the flesh is bondage to fear. But fear of what? Fear of not being enough and fear of not doing enough, yes, but I think the goodness gospel speaks to fear at a much deeper level. It actually makes us afraid of grace. We are afraid to let ourselves fall completely on the grace of Christ. *Surely*, we tell ourselves, *there is something more I have to do to please God. Surely I must keep myself in line. Surely I must prove myself to him. Surely I must be good in order for him to bless me. Surely I must do what other Christians around me are doing. Surely there is a point where God's grace cannot go.*

In a similar vein, the goodness gospel promotes a distrust of too much grace. We want to err on the side of goodness, so we hold on to both the law and grace, believing we were saved by grace but it's the law that will keep us in line. So just to be safe, we try to hold on to both. But in reality there cannot be both. It's grace or it's law, as Paul makes clear:

> For if I build again those things which I destroyed [the law], I make myself a transgressor. For I through the law died to the law that I might live to God. (Gal. 2:18–19)

> But that no one is justified by the law in the sight of God is evident, for "the just shall live by faith." (3:11)

> For if there had been a law given which could have given life, truly righteousness would have been by the law. But the Scripture has confined all under sin, that the promise by faith in Jesus Christ might be given to those who believe. But before faith came, we were kept under guard by the law, kept for the faith which would afterward be revealed. Therefore the law was our tutor to bring us to Christ, that we might be justified by faith. But after faith has come, we are no longer under a tutor. (vv. 21–25)

In other words, we cannot live by both law and grace. The law teaches us that we need Christ, but after salvation the law excludes Christ.

Finally, the goodness gospel makes us afraid of giving others too much grace. When we're living in that paradigm and others fall, we have nothing to give them except judgment because we are so afraid of appearing to cheapen grace. When we live according to the goodness gospel, we don't trust God to do the work of sanctification in our hearts and we also don't trust him to do the work of sanctification in the hearts of other people. We are just as frustrated by the weaknesses and failures of other believers as we are with our own. We have no grace to give because we ourselves are not living in grace.

The Goodness Gospel Is Driven by the Need for Approval

The goodness gospel intently follows man-made rules and causes us to make decisions and evaluations about behavior based on man-made stipulations. We become followers of man and man-made religion, not followers of God.

We find evidence of this in Paul's interaction with the Galatians. Paul observed that the Galatians were being "zealously courted" by a certain faction in the church, called the Judaizers, who wanted to "exclude" Paul and his message so the Galatian believers would be "zealous for them." It appears the faction wanted the Galatians to be formed in their own image.

Paul was zealous for them too, but for very different things. He called them: "My little children, for whom I labor in birth again until *Christ is formed in you.*"[5] Do you see the difference? The Judaizers wanted the believers to follow their rules and their ideas for the sole reason of developing followers of themselves. Their legalism led them to make and observe man-made regulations, to hold certain people on a higher plane, and to despise those who questioned them. Paul, instead, wanted the believers to understand the truth of the gospel and to experience freedom through it, not for the purpose of developing followers for himself but for the purpose of those believers becoming more like Christ.

The goodness gospel leads us to act like the Judaizers and Galatians. When we attempt to follow certain guidelines for Christianity, we tend to become entangled in a constant desire to please others. If what we do outwardly is only for the benefit of others so they will view us as a "good Christian," then we can be sure we are missing what God is saying to us and asking us to do. We become followers of men, and our love and devotion are given to men while our duty and obligation are given to Christ. We are also driven to be like certain people and not Christ, and we are motivated by and followers of speakers, bloggers, authors, pastors, and teachers rather than Christ himself.

The Goodness Gospel Bears Bitter Fruit

Unfortunately, the effects of the goodness gospel are not solely individual and internal. It also leads to division and factions within the church. Paul experienced this by the Judaizers' attempt to lock him and his gospel out. He also had to call out church leaders who had gotten caught up in it.

> Now when Peter had come to Antioch, I withstood him to his face, because he was to be blamed; for before certain men came from James, he would eat with the Gentiles; but when they came, he withdrew and separated himself, fearing those who were of the circumcision. And the rest of the Jews also played the hypocrite with him, so that even Barnabas was carried away with their hypocrisy. (Gal. 2:11–13)

Peter was well known, especially among Jewish converts, and was considered a prominent man in early Christianity, leading us to assume that he exerted tremendous influence among the early church. He had been serving and living among the Gentile converts, but suddenly, upon the arrival of church leaders from James's church in Jerusalem, he backed away from the Gentiles and began associating only with the Jewish believers. Evidently, those from James's church were not being taught to leave their Jewish ordinances behind, reflected in their interactions with those in Antioch. In other words, they were encouraging, by their own practices, the Jewish converts to continue in the law.

Peter, being an influential leader and a former Jew himself, most likely felt pressure to look good in the eyes of his visitors and to conform to his old ways of religion. A return to those old ways would have immediately set up a wall between Christian believers in the church: those who came from a Jewish background and those who came from a Gentile background. So Peter, in his attempt to please certain people and appear spiritual in the eyes of his visitors, caused division among the body of Christ.

Unfortunately, the same principle holds true in some of our churches today. When we subscribe to the belief that we have to carry out specific actions in order to be a good Christian, it inevitably results in division among Christians. We begin to categorize believers according to what they do.

When we ourselves live from the goodness gospel, we view and judge others according to what they do, not by the grace of Christ. When instead we understand that every believer is covered by the grace of God and adopted as his child, *just as we are*, we no longer categorize or label believers but love each the same. When grace abounds, the divisions in the church fall away. This is why Paul says, "Therefore, from now on, we regard no one according to the flesh . . . if anyone is in Christ, he is a new creation; old things have passed away; behold, all things have become new" (2 Cor. 5:16–17).

Stand Firm

Now that we recognize the symptoms of our goodness obsession and see where it leads us, we must cling all the more to the cross of Christ and let his grace reign in our lives. Paul exhorts the Galatians, and us, to stand firm in this freedom for which we've been made free and not be moved or swayed by anything that is not the gospel of grace.[6] How do we manage this on a daily basis, when we're assailed from every angle by claims on our identity and actions that are based on a weak gospel?

We must continue as we started. "As you therefore have received Christ Jesus the Lord, so walk in Him" (Col. 2:6). And how is it that we began? Christ called, we accepted the offer of new life, we died with him, and we rose with him to follow God as a new creation. Our only work was to believe, receive, and respond to his leadership.[7]

So if we are to continue just as we started, we should persevere in this way. He calls to us daily to remain in our new reality and dwell delightfully on all the glorious riches of Christ. We must respond to his call. We will stay dead to our old reality only by allowing the Holy Spirit to lead and work in us rather than returning to human effort to attempt to produce spiritual fruit. And just as we recognized his pursuit of us for salvation and relented to his work in our hearts by faith, we must trust his pursuit of us for sanctification and relent to him daily so that he may sanctify us completely.[8]

Just as we received at the start, God longs for us to receive from him each day. Christ has ended our slavery to the law, made us sons and daughters, given us the Spirit, procured our intimacy with God, and made us heirs of God and his own coheirs. He did all this willingly and joyfully. Should he not want us to flee from the goodness gospel and simply *enjoy* him and the freedom he brings on a daily basis?

We must keep moving forward by faith, clinging to grace, and following the leading of the Spirit, continuing to work out our salvation by *receiving*. We must never move away from the simplicity that is in Christ.[9] Let us stand firm in the grace of Christ that has made us free, and he will do the work in our hearts that we desire.

As we've considered what God wants for us and from us, it raises a question: Is this—the simplicity of the gospel—what we are concerned with? Or are we more like Martha, anxious and worried about many things? Martha's goodness addiction led to distraction, false urgency, inner turmoil, comparison, irritability, and misplaced blame on both Jesus and Mary.

I imagine Jesus took Martha's face in his hands and spoke her name with compassion and grace, just like my husband does when he speaks into my frazzled state by reminding me of the simple, core truth of grace. With Martha's face in his hands, Jesus called her to come and follow, but also to come and receive. With food cooking and a house full of guests with needs, Jesus brought Martha back to what matters: following and receiving before giving, following and receiving so that she *could* give something of significance to others. After all, we cannot give away anything unless we have received it first.

Because Jesus values dependence and faith rather than self-made goodness and accomplishment, the gospel also frees us from the ever-growing expectations of performance in our world. He invites us to accept a new paradigm of redemption and, with it, an identity that he's crafted for us.

I like to think I am creating my identity or, in a sense, creating who I am known as or will be remembered as. My daily efforts and energies go toward crafting this identity: Christine the wife, mother, minister, writer. I not only want to be identified by these roles but also be known as good at them. Christine: good wife, good mother, good minister, good writer. But my attempts to craft an identity apart from what Christ wants to form in me—how *he* wants to shape these roles that, ultimately, are gifts he's given and controls—are often self-gratifying and self-indulgent. When crafted and honed apart from God, they are always lacking and unfulfilling, because I could always be doing more or doing better. Crafting and maintaining an identity apart from Christ is a losing, bitter game.

The apostle Paul could have identified himself by any number of roles: intellectual, apostle, writer, itinerant preacher, evangelist. He, however, ran and hid in Christ, allowing God's definition of who he was to become his own: called, beloved, separated. He self-identified only as a lowly bondservant, his every action, word, and breath wrapped up completely in the gospel.

I just stick to the labels that form my everyday life.

But *what if?* What if we stopped pouring our energies into crafting an identity of our own that reflects well on us? What if we cared less about impressing others with a specially honed image? What if we instead allowed God's definition of us to become how we define ourselves? How might it change our days if we identified ourselves as called, beloved, separated?

If we are *called*, and we are in Christ, then we are pursued and wooed. We have been invited to belong as coheirs with Christ. We are also invited each day to remain in this belonging. What else or who else can compare with such an invitation?

If we are *beloved*, and we are in Christ, then we are dearly loved. Our belonging is never in question and neither is God's love toward us. In fact, his love is generously and delightfully given. What else or who else can compare with such a love?

If we are *separated*, and we are in Christ, our "in Christness" grants us a new identity, different than the one we had apart from him. We are divided out into his family and have taken on his name. What else or who else can compare with such a gift?

The driving core of all he calls and makes us is the gospel. It has changed us, it keeps us, and it continues to regenerate us as we remain in Christ. Much like my college ID card gave me access to things I needed and wanted as a student, the identity he's lavished us with gives us access to the glorious riches of God himself.

If we will just receive.

But how?

Part Two

From Good to Grace

Receiving

Therefore, since we are receiving a kingdom which cannot be shaken, let us have grace.

Hebrews 12:28

4

Receiving His Love

LAST MOTHER'S DAY, my husband gave me porcelain name plates (Writeable! Erasable! Dishwasher safe!) for entertaining, and I squealed and kissed his face. My mind raced with the many uses I could squeeze from such a gift: place cards for holiday dinners, labels for indecipherable-to-the-naked-eye potluck casseroles, and tags for distinguishing between the decaf and the fully loaded.

While I exuded excitement, my husband stood stunned and amazed that, having spent just a few dollars, he'd hit the gift-giving jackpot. He knew I loved to throw parties, but he didn't know just how *much* until I unwrapped those name plates.

I *do* love to throw a party, and I love anything that might help me throw a great party: silverware caddies, drink dispensers, ice buckets, serving dishes, pitchers, and beautiful bowls. And platters! I'm a sucker for platters.

I love to throw a party, but, even more, I love when guests relish parties and dinners in my home, not because it's in my home or because I'm such a great host with phenomenal platters, but because I want the people that I love, and even those I'm just getting to know, to feel special. It makes me happy when they relax, when they let me serve them, and when they delight in the food and the company of the other guests. My most joyful moments as a host occur when the conversation is flowing, the laughter is easy, and everyone is clearly content to be with one another.

As you can imagine, when I read passages in Scripture equating heaven as a wedding ceremony followed by a great big dinner party, I get really excited. My mouth waters when I envision the food and drink. My heart skips a beat as I attempt to picture the décor and the environment. And the platters! I can't even go there. Heavenly, literally.

But the best part by far, I envision, will be the company. Perhaps you and I will dine together, surrounded by friends, family, and people we didn't know on this earth but who are at once fascinating and intimate companions. All of us sitting and feasting at the dinner party to end all dinner parties. Together we will raise a glass to toast our Host, the God of the universe, at the head of the table. Together we will enjoy him.

Let's turn our attention to him now and consider: In that moment when his children are finally gathered home, when the world of sin and death has passed away, when faith is sight—what will God enjoy? It seems to me that, like any good party host, he will enjoy us receiving the feast and the home he has prepared for us. He will enjoy us enjoying one another. He will enjoy serving us, and seeing our delight at finally being with him. He will celebrate, and we'll follow his lead.

When I think of God delighting as he throws us a really good party, it surprises me a little, like I've got him wrong. Does that sit a little funny with you too? Does it feel a little sacrilegious? If so, perhaps we're missing that God is in fact a celebratory God and he delights and exults in those who accept his invitation to come to the party and sit at his table. If we miss the very salient fact that God is a celebratory God, I think we miss who he really is, and I think we're in danger of being a bad party guest.

As a host, I've experienced bad party guests. Some don't RSVP but come anyway, they show up way too late or leave way too early, they don't engage others in conversation, or they talk too much about themselves. But what really makes a bad party guest is someone who frets over being served, as if they don't deserve it or they have to create a good reason for their having been invited. When they can't relax and receive, they take from my joy as their host.

Even now, as we have not yet experienced the kingdom of heaven but are experiencing a morsel of the feast to come, God is the consummate host. It is his nature and character to serve, and, as his followers, he wants us to receive from and respond to his lead. We are certainly not honored above him, as if we deserve his attention and service, but we honor him when we receive and relish the grace, love, and joy that he purchased for us.

Many of us are party poopers in relation to our celebratory God. We bring a pitiful good-works casserole when the invitation clearly stated all was taken care of. We cower in the corner like a wallflower, afraid we don't belong, that our invitation was an accident. Or we hop up to replenish our own drinks or to clear away the dishes rather than focusing on the relationships at the table, especially with the One sitting in the head seat.

If we take our eyes off our own insecurities, if we stop striving to be good for a moment, and look at the Host, we find that he is delighted to have us at the table, and he is delighted most as we enjoy the love and grace he's giving. His eyes are dancing to the rhythm of his creation; he hopes we notice its beauty as well. His heart is full as he watches his children enjoy each other's company and delight in their Host together. He reaches out to us with gentle affection and turns his ear to listen to our cares, concerns, and joys. There is peace and hope and communion aplenty to be had here.

As You Received, Continue to Receive

If we are followers of Christ, we are the guests sitting at God's table. You're there, and I'm there, and how did we get here? It's quite simple actually: he invited and we said yes. He offered, we received. He saw our need and offered a rescue; we saw our need too and came with only despair, desire, and faith. We accepted the invitation, we were brought to the table, and the despair we've felt over our sin was flung out the door by the divine bouncer himself, Jesus Christ.

Most of us get this. We may not have realized it was a party and that it's supposed to be joy-filled, but we understand we've accepted a blood-wrought invitation. For many, however, we're not sure what is expected next. We're quite certain we didn't get here on our own merit, but now that we're here, we don't know how to be good party guests at God's table. We goodness-obsessed don't know how to enjoy God. And we definitely don't know how to receive his enjoyment of us unless we're doing something to earn it. We simply don't know how to receive his love, even though it's the one thing we need to know and *want* to know every day.

Paul was a guy who got it, which is mind-blowing considering the life he lived, hunting Christians, before God revealed himself in such dramatic fashion.

One way Paul identifies himself in Scripture is as the "called" of Jesus Christ, who is separated to Christ and his gospel.[1] Often, we associate the word "called" with a vocation or activity, as in we are "called to ministry" or "called to adopt" or "called to be a teacher." But Paul says all believers are called—called to be saints.[2] Does our vocation or activity make us saints? No, only Christ makes uo oaintoꞈ thorofore, wo aro called to him. We are called to receive from him our sainthood, our seat at the table, our entry into what Paul calls the Beloved.[3] We are a part of a people characterized as loved by God. That's why Paul, despite his past, got it; he identified himself as loved. Do we identify ourselves as loved? We should, because Christ has pursued us, wooed us, invited us, and made us beloved to the Father.

Paul also made it clear that our response to the initial invitation is no different than our response once we're at the table: "As you therefore have received Christ Jesus the Lord, so walk in Him" (Col. 2:6). In other words, just as we received the invitation to the table by faith, we are to continue receiving from Christ each day by faith. We are to stand firm in the grace by which we've been made free,[4] not tarnish that grace by foolishly attempting to prove we're meant to be at the table or tread on it by steering the conversation back to our own accomplishments and glory.

For many, the idea that we just sit back and receive is uncomfortable. Shouldn't we be doing something? We'll discover later in this book that, yes, our Host will send us out to talk about him and show him and bring others to the table, but *even in that* we are receivers. He gives us our competency for the task, and the gifts and talents with which to do it. He does the work of producing spiritual fruit. It's easy for us to turn quickly to a task list of response because we innately feel as if we must *do* something rather than *be* and *receive*. But before we turn to our response, we must clarify that receiving is the most important part.

When Jesus took the towel and basin to the feet of his disciples, at a celebratory dinner feast no less, he did so out of love: "having loved His own who were in the world, He loved them to the end" (John 13:1). He showed this love by serving, and he served in a shocking manner: washing feet caked in dust from the street. This was the lowliest servant's job. His love and service to them was extravagant.

Initially, Peter refused to have his feet washed, feeling unworthy, just as we sometimes refuse to believe the extent of the love and service God has shown us in Christ, and just as we feel more comfortable in the serving position. Jesus, however, said plainly, "If I do not wash you, you have no part with Me" (v. 8). He meant more than their feet, of course. He indicated that their hearts could only be purified if they received what he offered. We too *must* learn to receive love from him or we have no communion with God. In fact, if there is something we must be "good" at as Christians, it's receiving God's love.

It's just wild, the extent and extravagance of this love that we've received and that is available for us to receive on a daily basis. We have done nothing to earn this invitation, yet we are seated among the saints. We received this extravagant, feet-washing love at salvation, but we are invited to continue receiving it every day after.

What Is the Love We're Receiving?

What is God's love like? What does it do? How do we recognize it? How are we to think about it? Answering these questions will go far in helping us receive it.

At one point in my life, I asked these questions because I couldn't juxtapose suffering and God's discipline with his love. How could his love remain silent or allow his children to go to the deepest depths of their stubborn sin?

Sometimes it's hard for me to see that God is love. Perhaps that's because my definition of love so often contradicts the true definition of love.

I wrestled with these questions because I watched a friend leave the Lord and go her own way. No matter my words and the words of others, no matter my prayers, no matter the fasting and prayers of our faith community, she didn't return.

That year of struggle and wrestling felt like one long, barren winter. Spring birthed the cherry blossoms lining the city's main thoroughfare, summer delivered a blanket of humidity, fall dazzled with oranges and yellows and ambers—but still, winter remained. A heart in winter, my heart, knew well the thin, bare tree limbs, the snow-capped silence, the bitter cold, the longing for new life.

My friend was gone, hearts were breaking, and only questions remained.

Would it be an endless winter?

Had God been defeated?

Was he strong enough to change a heart?

And the biggest question of all: How was he showing love in this situation?

I needed winter to thaw into spring. I needed hope and restoration, true and beautiful. As the prodigal's brother, I needed the Father's heart. Most of all, I needed a renewed picture of love. Not fleeting, shifting, romantic love, but love that withstands the burdens and pressures and failings and sufferings and needs of the entire world. Love that holds up. Perfect love, unadulterated by a limited human perspective.

Of course, I knew *about* God. Certainly, I could list his attributes and state facts about how he acts—all the things I knew I *should* believe about him. But did I know him? Specifically, did I know how he loves? What is this love? How does this love act? How does this love respond? How is this love expressed? How is this love experienced? Do I know this Person, Jesus, who thinks, wills, feels, and acts love toward the world and toward me?

I needed to know. Desperately and passionately, I needed to know. My heart cried out for God's deep and abiding love to come and transition my heart from winter to spring. I needed to know how to enjoy God, and I needed to know that he enjoyed me.

Perhaps you need to know this love too. I imagine that you know about God, and you can roughly paraphrase the main points of

Scripture and/or theology. I imagine that you are a dutiful person, trying to live life right. You take your friends meals when they have babies, and you make sure your kids have clean socks. You go to church, you pay your bills, and you give to the needy at Christmas. A few times a week, you sit down to read your Bible because you know it's good for you, but you often desire more out of that time. Late at night, when you can't sleep, you wonder if you're just going through the motions, if there is any of the promised abundance in all this rote, mundane, religious life. Mostly, you wonder if God truly loves you, if you are good enough for him, or if you're doing enough for him. You wonder if you have a seat at the table and if the Host is delighted to enjoy your company. More than anything in all the world, you long to know God, have a deep relationship with him, and comprehend his approval.

I know you.

I know you because I know me.

What I've discovered is that if we look for his love in all the right places, it is available to us to understand and receive. We can actually grab hold of and enjoy the love of God.

A. W. Tozer's statement in *The Pursuit of God* has inspired me to deeply explore the Bible for characteristics and outworkings of God's love:

> For it is not mere words that nourish the soul, but God himself, and unless and until the hearers find God in personal experience they are not the better for having heard the truth. The Bible is not an end in itself, but a means to bring men to an intimate and satisfying knowledge of God, that they may enter into him, that they may delight in his Presence, may taste and know the inner sweetness of the very God himself in the core and center of their hearts.[5]

And so I searched every book of the Bible, not for knowledge that puffs up or special insight, but for God himself. I looked for how he loves his people so that I could recognize and receive it myself, and so I could love like him, especially in the heartache I was experiencing. What I found is that his love permeates every page, every story, every part of his plan. This shouldn't have come as a surprise, because if God is love, then love must be where he is.

I also realized quickly that it is not humanly possible to comprehensively describe the fullness, the outworking, and the complexities of God's love because his love is so completely unlike the imperfect love we share with one another. I certainly do not think I will be able to sum up the love of God for you in this chapter.

But I believe that God's love (and anything about him, for that matter) has facets, much like a skyscraper. If we try to look at it as a whole, it is difficult to take it all in or to see the details that make it what it is. But if we explore the details, go floor to floor, and look at the building from various angles, we piece together an accurate picture of the skyscraper. We *know* the skyscraper.

We have a lifetime to explore God's love in Scripture, to look at it from every angle we can, and to try to taste both its bitterness (the death of Christ for us) and its sweetness (our adoption as sons and daughters). What I've found is that exploring God's love always lifts our eyes away from ourselves and onto him. His love says nothing about us—that we are somehow lovable or worthy to be the object of his love—but everything about the goodness and graciousness of our God. He loved us when we were still far off, when we despised and rejected him. He loves with *agape* love, a love that is given without any expectation of return.

His love lifts our eyes onto him but it also leads us to respond. We search for him and for his love so we might know him and receive his love but also so we might respond in grateful worship.

What I discovered is that the facets of God's love touch every aspect of love that we know and experience between one another, but his love is the fulfillment or perfection of the love we experience as broken or imperfect. Righteous earthly love is but a taste of the love of God.

What exactly does this love look like? First of all, we cannot talk about true love without talking about God. God and love are interchangeable, a definitive equation where one equals the other. Because God equals love, we can surmise that love is his character—it's who he is. He consists of love. Because he is love, his will toward us is loving. He wills that we experience his love and love him and others in return.

The Bible says we can see and understand the love of God based upon the words and deeds of Jesus Christ. His life displays how God's love is shown toward us.

It is demonstrative toward us. He showed it by dying for us—and not just dying, but dying for us before we could do anything to try to make ourselves worthy of it. We did nothing to bring ourselves to the table.[6]

It is the ultimate love. There is no greater demonstration of love than to die for someone who hates you, and that's precisely what Jesus did.[7] This type of love seems almost foolish in nature, that's how wild and celebratory it is.

It is a heroic and provisionary love. Christ took our licks for us, appeasing God's just wrath toward our sin.[8] There is no fear or timidity needed at God's table, because Christ has earned our belonging.

It is a love that mends. Christ brings us into reconciliation with the Father so that we can have unending relationship with him. This is a love that leads to rejoicing, not repayment.[9]

A Picture of His Love

To understand God's love, I need more than statements like that, however. I'm a visual learner, so I learn from word pictures. My favorite word picture for God's love, the one that helps me know what it means to receive it, is the word picture for redemption.

Redemption means "to buy back" or "to reclaim ownership,"[10] as you might buy a slave to set him free.

There is a great deal of history packed into the little city where I live, including Thomas Jefferson's home, the courthouse where he practiced law, and the place of commissioning for the Lewis and Clark expedition.

It is not all history to be proud of, however.

There is a corner near the courthouse square where slaves were at one time auctioned off to the highest bidder. I've stood there countless times, reading the commemorative plaque, looking out toward the square, imagining how scary and unjust it would have been to be enslaved and auctioned as property, thinking about the lengths we humans go to hurt one another.

And then I think of Ruth in the Bible.

The book of Ruth illustrates God's love toward us using the word *redeemer*, which we've already learned is a word linked to being freed from slavery. The book of Ruth is not typically associated with slavery. Instead, we think of it as similar to our modern-day Christian romance novels with their damsels in distress and their dashing heroes coming to the rescue. When we read this sweet Old Testament book, we pronounce God to be the ultimate matchmaker, stamp *And they lived happily ever after* on the last line, and close our Bible with a contented, pining sigh.

It is true that Ruth is a love story in all those ways, but if we stop there and don't dig deeper, we miss God himself and how he loves. This picture—the underlying treasure of Ruth—isn't soft and sweet like a romance. This picture involves women of questionable character, poverty, hopelessness, idol worship, secret agendas, intrigue, and a woman proposing marriage to a man. In other words, it is nothing like our modern-day Christian romance novels.

First, a little background: Ruth was a Moabite woman. She married into an Israelite family when they sought to escape into her country from the famine that was God's discipline. Moabites were generally despised by the Israelites because they were distant cousins who had turned away from the Lord into pagan beliefs and practices, including using sexual acts to worship false gods. Because of these practices, Moabite women were especially despised; they were considered seductive and loose. No self-respecting, God-fearing Israelite would have anything to do with them.

Ruth was one of those women. There is no telling what she experienced prior to her marriage and her subsequent departure to Judah with Naomi when their husbands died. She certainly would not have been welcomed and accepted when she moved into a town filled with Israelites. Without a husband, she was stuck, seemingly hopeless, lacking provision or protection. Derided by the people around her, she would have had daily reminders of her past, despite her decision to follow Israel's God.

Although not literally a slave, she lived much like a slave. A slave to her past. A slave to the cultural system where a woman was helpless without a man. A slave to poverty. She was a cast-aside, a lesser-than.

But then, Boaz. *Thankfully*, Boaz. Our hero, Boaz, stepped in and took her as his wife. He was what was then called a kinsman redeemer, a close relative who redeemed or bought back something that belonged to the family. Aside from being a close relative, the kinsman redeemer had to be able to pay the price and be willing to reclaim ownership.[11] In the Old Testament, redemption was applied to property, animals, and even the nation of Israel as a whole, but in Ruth's case it was applied to a person.

Boaz, by redeeming Ruth, purchased a figurative freedom for her. When he redeemed her, the weight of her past, her reputation, and her poverty lifted immediately. He rescued her.

But if we make this story all about Ruth and Boaz, we miss the larger love story, the foreshadowing of a future Redeemer who would purchase freedom for all the world.

Christ is our Kinsman Redeemer: he is related because he became man, he was able to pay the price for our sins because he lived a perfect life, and he was willing to do so through his own death.

And so the word picture demonstrates how God has loved us and loves us still. Like Ruth, we've known slavery—spiritual slavery apart from Christ. We've been the ones standing in a figurative cage, being watched and humiliated by a crowd of demonic mockers who know our worst days and our worst stories. We've stood destitute in our sin. We've been without hope.

But then, Jesus. *Thankfully*, Jesus.

Remember when you were without hope? Remember your chains of have-to legalism and sin? Or perhaps you're still very much in your chains because you've never accepted the invitation Jesus offers. Perhaps your feelings indict you and keep you in that cage, even though the door is open and the chains are unlocked. Perhaps you are skittish to abandon yourself to True Love because you've been mocked, abused, and hurt by lesser lovers.

Stand with me on the corner and turn to face the square.

Look, here he comes! Though the crowd is murmuring, look up. He is pushing his way through until he reaches your cage. He wraps his hands urgently around the bars. Don't be ashamed. Don't try to cover yourself, don't try to make yourself or your life look more presentable, because you cannot. Look into his eyes and see that he looks at you differently than the crowd does. This is the look of One who knows you intimately, because he created you. The tenderness and compassion in his eyes will make you stand a little taller, hope a little harder.

Now, look. Without hesitation, he is paying for you by giving himself. Your captor has no choice; he is powerless now, he must unlock the cage. Jesus is taking your hand and leading you away from your cage, away from who you once were. Go with him! He will lead you to his home, not to be a slave but to sit at the table with him as a daughter, to enjoy the comfort and warmth of the feast. There, he will give you his name and rich, beautiful clothes of righteousness. Best of all, he will give himself to you. Because he loves you. *That's the only reason he would do such a thing.* Receive that wild, extravagant, joyful love.

This is redemption. This is love, yet *just one facet* of a larger love.

If you are in Christ, this is a picture of what he has done for you. He has redeemed you. You are no longer the Moabite woman enslaved to your past. You are no longer the outcast. You are no longer at sin's mercy. You don't have to cover yourself with attempts at perfection. You don't have to cover yourself in shame any longer. You are no longer a slave but are now his daughter.

This is Ruth's story, and this is ours: we have been redeemed with a redeeming love.

No Longer Orphans

Our redemption occurred at the point in time when we put our faith in Jesus, and while it is helpful to look back with gratefulness, we need to know how God's love applies each day. We need to know God's love for us in the midst of laundry, hurts, mundane tasks, and struggles.

Again, to help me understand God's love in my daily life, I turn to a word picture. It comes from Galatians 4:4–5: "God sent forth his Son, born of a woman, born under the law, to *redeem* those who were under the law, that we might *receive the adoption* as sons [and daughters]."

In Christ, because of the redemption he has purchased for me, I am no longer an orphan but a daughter. He brings me to God's table not as an outside guest but as an adopted member of the family.

To understand this more fully, consider the life of an orphan. An orphan has to take care of herself; she has no one looking out for her. An orphan must be strong and protect herself from being taken advantage of or hurt. She can't depend on anyone, and she also can't be weak. An orphan craves to be taken in and loved but doubts she ever will be. An orphan wants to belong to a family; she wants to be accepted. She is afraid to get too close, afraid that she will never truly be loved. An orphan is on the outside looking in.

Does this not describe us when we live according to the goodness gospel? We have to be self-sufficient, strong, self-protective, and independent. Why? Because we doubt we are truly loved by God.

In reality, God's love for us means that we are no longer orphans but adopted daughters who are coheirs with Christ. Because we are no longer orphans, we don't have to live like orphans, doubting that we have a Father who loves us and provides for us. We can live every day as daughters, being dependent on our perfect Father, being vulnerable in our weakness so that he can be strong, and receiving and relishing our belonging in the Beloved.

Receiving God's Love Poured Out

We are redeemed *from* our sin but we are also redeemed *for* God. We are freed from slavery but we now belong to the One who purchased us with his blood:

> For none of us lives to himself, and no one dies to himself. For if we live, we live to the Lord; and if we die, we die to the Lord. Therefore, whether we live or die, we are the Lord's. For to this end Christ died and rose and lived again. (Rom. 14:7–9)

To receive God's love is to receive Christ as he meant for us to receive him, living as belonging to Christ and no longer to ourselves. His love is free; it's extravagant but it cannot be trampled on or demanded to bend according to our desires. This isn't a love that we can control; we can't keep him from loving those we think are unlovable. This isn't a love we earn as we feed our goodness obsession. This isn't a love relationship between equals in which we command God in how his love should be shown. This isn't a love that is always going to make us comfortable and happy; indeed, he will compel us to love like him and forgive like him and sacrifice like him. As he is a servant, he will lead us to service.

To receive his love daily means to die to ourselves daily—to release any rights we think we have to ourselves—so that we might give ourselves to him and enjoy him. After all, we can't hold out hands to receive while also clinging tightly to our own agendas, ambitions, and dreams of self-glory.

But when God's love is received as he gives it, he indeed makes us free. How is it that we belong to another but are also considered free? This is a question that assumes rulership is negative, harsh, and demanding, when in fact self-rule is the rule that leads to enslavement and death. God-rule is *always* just, right, and good. He gives freedom because his rule is our perfect protection.

This is what it means that God is jealous for us: he wants us to receive freedom and joy, and he indeed knows where this is rightly found—as we submit ourselves to his rule. This is one of the great paradoxes of Christianity, perhaps because we bristle under any authority and innately value self-rule most of all. But God doesn't rule as a Master who needs and demands; he rules as a loving Father leading his household, taking joyful responsibility for the well-being of his family. He invites us to enjoy the very best, which is himself and the communal feast around his table. Until we receive his love as he gives it—freely, without expectation of return—and let him lead us to his celebratory table, we have an awfully hard time seeing how belonging to him is also our freedom.

In the end, he leaves the decision to us. We get the party to which we accept the invitation: self-rule (including our efforts to be good) leading to death, or God-rule leading to life forever. God is passionate and jealous for us to accept the only good invitation. Will we receive it as he gives it?

What I'm trying to say is that God loves you. He is jealous for you, and the invitation to redemption is for you. If you are in Christ, you have been redeemed. You sit at the table as a daughter. And this is perhaps the best part: in this reality where grace reigns, you delight God because Christ delights God, and when God looks at you, he sees Christ in your place. You have his approval because Christ has his approval. This is your reality this very moment, and it will be your reality tomorrow and forever.

Stop stiff-arming this truth because you're afraid you're unworthy. Is Jesus unworthy of God's love and approval? Is Jesus condemned and guilt-laden? Then you aren't either.

Accept it by faith.

Receive it by faith.

Because that's what God wants for you more than anything else—more than all your good works combined, more than you reading your Bible from cover to cover, more than you giving all your money and possessions away. He wants you to receive the gift he was delighted to give, and to look into your salvation every day, and to enjoy it, and to let that love sink in so it will well up and lead to response.

Quit worrying about the response before receiving his love. Quit fretting that you'll trample on grace before even letting it sink into your heart. The table we've been invited to is a table of holiness and righteousness, yes, but we don't make ourselves that way. Christ makes us holy and righteous, and as we receive his love, our response will include dying daily so that we might awaken to righteousness.[12] We will make no provision for the flesh because we desire to live according to the Spirit. This is the heart's desire of the redeemed. To be loved is to want to love back, and the way we love him back is to awaken to what pleases him.

God's love is an everyday reality for the believer, made possible by Christ. God made us alive out of his good pleasure and kindness, but it was not one-time kindness.[13] This is perpetual kindness; he continues to show us the exceeding riches of his grace and kindness toward us in Christ. We, then, must continue to look into our salvation. We must continue to walk with him and receive the love he gives.

In order to grasp what we can of God's love, we must be "rooted and grounded" in it (Eph. 3:17). If we are rooted and grounded in God's love, it means that it is the basis and foundation for all that we do and think. In other words, we must return each day to the cross with relentless faith and relentless focus, praying, as Paul did, that we could know what is beyond our rational knowing.

His love must never be in doubt. Sometimes we will experience God's love as intimate and sure. But sometimes we will experience God's love as discipline because he is a good Father who brings us back to where we can receive his love and experience true freedom. Sometimes we will experience God's love as bittersweet, knowing that he is allowing sin's consequences so that we will return to him. Sometimes we will experience God's love as impartial because he will ask us to forgive someone who has offended us, just as he forgives them and forgives us. And sometimes we will experience God's love as companion love because we feel alone and he is all we have.

But when we know God is love *always*, we can trust that his interactions, responses, and requests of us are all from a heart of love toward us.

What if we are afraid to go to Jesus with boldness and confidence? What if we doubt we are truly loved and welcomed at God's table? What if we still feel we must prove that we're worth it?

The way God intends for us to receive his gifts, including his love, is through faith. There is no rational way of understanding the extent and immensity of God's love for us—that's like trying to picture the ocean (or the skyscraper) in its entirety. There is only faith—a stubborn refusal to look away from Christ as the basis for God's love toward us. To receive God's love by faith means to *not* try to receive it by other things. accomplishments, self-sufficiency, the validation of others. It means we don't refuse it because of any fear, irrational self-talk, guilt, or circumstances. It means we don't find security in anything other than Christ. We put no confidence in the flesh, ours or anyone else's. There is nothing outward or of ourselves that we depend on. Living by faith means that we believe and live by the truth that God never asked us to be good but rather asked us to be holy like he is holy, and that the holiness he gives and grows in us is the holiness he asks for. Living by faith is an assurance of our standing with God in Christ and an assurance that this standing will never change.

Oh sweet assurance, Jesus is ours.

And we are his.

Love That Leads

I prayed myself through the winter of my heartbreak, holding on by faith, pleading with God for his love to come through. That winter, the trees outside my window drooped under the weight of ice and, inside, fire warmed my chilled bones. It was a cold, silent, barren winter.

But in my heart, spring came. New life and fresh joy poked up where the barrenness once was. Heartbreak remained but winter thawed, because of the love of God that I discovered in his Word. I'd known it for a while, but the filled-in gaps, the expanded details, and the illustrative stories sparked something new.

And I received it, letting him wash way down in the doubts and questions and defeat I felt. God's love has a way of doing that. It sinks in deep, touching parts of us that have gone fallow or that have hidden in darkness, driving out fear and shame. He reveals himself and then calls us even deeper, though we can never reach his end. God's love is infinitely greater than any definition or description we give it.

I relearned that trying to be good, whether as a Christian or as a mom or as a friend, simply points me right back to my sin, because I cannot be perfectly good and I don't always have the answers and I don't know what to do most of the time.

When I soaked in my redemption, however, and considered my seat at the table, it pointed to a good, holy God who went to such great lengths to get me here. I felt the protection of his sovereignty and the assurance of never having to be separated from his love, even though things go wrong in this world and brokenness is all around.

He is worthy. That's what I thought to myself. He is worthy: of my faith, of my response, of my life.

And isn't that the thing about love? When it is received, it creates a response.

I saw it in Ezra, how people worshiped without inhibition. In Exodus, I read about how the Israelites stored God's faithfulness in their hearts to share with the next generation. In Philemon, Christ's love and forgiveness bridged the gap between a slave and a slave owner. In 1 John, it was so adamantly clear: if we know God's love, we will love our brother.

Yes, when love is received, it creates a response.

We love because he first loved us.

5

Receiving His Help

MY FAVORITE PART OF VACATION is the *anticipation* of it, especially if the vacation is just my husband and me, a new place to explore, and the promise of good food and sound sleep. In preparation, I gorge myself on pictures of our destination, imagining and anticipating how deliciously relaxing our getaway will be.

I have a horrible habit, however. When my husband and I get to our destination, my anticipation of the vacation always turns to the anticipation, or more accurately the dread, of it ending. Every morning, my head still on the pillow, I do the countdown: *Only five more days. Only four more days. Only three more days.*

I suppose I do this because I'm trying to give myself a pep talk. *Only five more days! Make the most of today while you can! Enjoy every second and take it all in! A week from now you'll once again be deep in the laundry and lunches!*

I try to keep these thoughts to myself. One, because my husband doesn't share in my struggle to relax and enjoy a vacation. Two, because he thinks my countdown is morbid and depressing.

And, in reality, it *is* quite morbid and depressing, even though my goal is actually to have a good time. I suppose I'm so filled with the dread of returning to the routines of life that I can't receive what's literally right in front of me. I'm so focused on forcing myself to have fun that I'm not having any fun at all.

I promise I'm pleasant to be around. Promise. Just don't tell me how many days are left in the vacation because I will panic for a brief moment.

I've realized that forcing things is also my tendency in relation to God. To show him my dedication and determination, I want to immediately respond. I want to be instantly spiritually mature, and I'll make list after list of how I plan to get myself there. I don't want to sit still to receive like Mary; I want to run around honoring Jesus with my service like Martha. As a result, I live in the mode of sheer panic and frenzy, overanalyzing and overstriving. It's no wonder I am obsessed with being good.

And it's no wonder it's a common problem. Because we really do want to please God, but we're forcing it. We walk around like it's up to us to figure things out and get things right and finally get our lives in order.

Take, for instance, the last chapter.

A typical goodness-obsessed response is to make a list of things we plan to do in order to understand and receive God's love. Or put reminders in sticky notes all over our bathroom mirrors: "God is love!" "There is no condemnation for those who are in Christ (smiley face, heart, underline)!" Perhaps you are super-spiritual and made a plan to memorize a verse or—look at you—a whole passage. Here we are, trying to get it right, but we go right back to our self-sufficient ways, trying to force the fun, so to speak. *We will have fun, gosh darn it. We're having fun, right?* (Forced smile.)

Or I WILL figure out how it is that God loves me. There must be a formula somewhere for that.

We can't force fun, just like we can't force ourselves to "get" God's love. That's like trying to corral and contain an ocean with an eyedropper.

You Can't Do It

Why do we do this? The answer is simple: we're fearful. We want control, and the idea that we can't intellectualize or force God's hand or force our own understanding of God's love is frustrating. We also fear we'll miss something we're supposed to do, we'll appear to not be good enough, or we'll disappoint God.

Think about it: most of the things we fear in life are things our emotions are acknowledging we're not actually in control over. We want to believe we have control over hearts, have control over circumstances, and can bring change. We tend to believe that we're responsible for a lot of things, our relationship with God primary among them.

It would be much simpler to slap some rules down and call it a day, but following rules and forcing righteousness through self-sufficiency is not life-giving. "For if there had been a law given which could have given life, truly righteousness would have been by the law" (Gal. 3:21). Self-sufficiency can't give life, and it doesn't.

But we believe otherwise, thank you very much. Our goodness-obsessed little hearts believe, fully and completely, that if we just work hard enough we can actually fulfill what Jesus commanded when he said, "Be perfect, just as your Father in heaven is perfect" (Matt. 5:48). Armed with our colored Sharpies and excellent work ethic, we take it as a challenge, not as an indictment that we aren't actually able.

We hold so tightly to our own capabilities, to our attempts at knowing God through a list of rules, because it's a little scary to let go, receive, and respond as he leads.

There is a wild, unruly aspect of identifying with Christ because we must set down the easily calculated checklist of the law and follow Someone whom we can't see and often can't feel and whom we all the time have trouble wrapping our minds around.

Also, in identifying with Christ, we're asked to do and be things that are impossible. Forgive an offender? Flee the lusts of the flesh? Be joyful always? Do everything without complaining?

If you're still ticking off items on your good-Christian checklist and haven't figured it out yet, let me tell you a little secret. There is a huge disclaimer to the Christian life, a disclaimer that for some reason most of us goodness-obsessed people have missed or have decidedly ignored. Here it is: the Christian life really *is* impossible. Those nagging thoughts questioning your own ability, which follow every sermon you hear or book you read or exhortation from a friend or command in the Word? Those thoughts are true—*you can't do it!* You are not competent for the task. You can sticky-note verses all you want, but that's not going to make you adequate to live the Christian life.

This may be a revelation to you. You may need to take a few deep breaths or spend a few moments gathering yourself in the quiet space among the color-sorted clothes in your closet. But, truly, think about it. As followers of Christ, we are asked to die to ourselves and take up his cross. He asks us to go against our very nature and embrace a life contrary to who we innately are. He asks a selfish and self-centered people to love and serve without expectation of return. He asks us to suffer with joy. He asks things of us that we cannot possibly do: be holy as he is holy, crucify our flesh with its passions and desires, put all our hope in an unseen reality.

The things God asks of those who follow Christ are attitudes and actions that involve the heart, a place that we can't reach and can't change, no matter our effort or desire.

Now that I've thoroughly discouraged you, I have another little secret. It's not so much a secret as it is a misapplied or underapplied truth: God gives us what we need to live the Christian life, and he gives it in the form of himself. He dwells inside the believer and, if we allow him to, lives the Christian life for us!

When Jesus was about to die, he said—and this is so amazing that I can hardly stand it—"It is *to your advantage* that I go away; for if I do not go away, the Helper will not come to you" (John 16:7). To our advantage? Who is this Helper who could possibly be better than Jesus in the flesh, talking to us, physically leading us, doing miracles right in front of us?

This helper is the Holy Spirit.

Who Is This Helper?

In the church I grew up in, we never talked about the Holy Spirit. For years into my adulthood, anytime anyone mentioned the Holy Spirit I got a little fidgety and nervous. I'd seen the Holy Spirit misrepresented and even misused, and I'd known that he (it?) was Someone (something?) often talked about in hushed tones or ignored completely. This very much explains my personal struggle through legalism and spiritual perfectionism because those who are led by the Spirit are not under the law, and, clearly, I lived under the law and under the law alone.[1] To my detriment, I was ignoring the Holy Spirit.

If we are to live by faith and in grace rather than by our own goodness, we cannot ignore the Holy Spirit. He is God, and just as we can't talk about love without talking about him, we can't talk about freedom without talking about him. Where the Spirit of the Lord is, there is liberty.[2] We can't talk about love and joy and peace without talking about him, because he is the One who produces those things in our hearts.[3] And, interestingly enough, we can't talk about goodness without talking about him, because goodness is a fruit of the Spirit. So let's talk about him: What is the Holy Spirit's role in our lives?

The Holy Spirit is who makes us competent for the Christian life.

Not that we are sufficient of ourselves to think of anything as being from ourselves, but our sufficiency is from God, who also made us sufficient as ministers of the new covenant, not of the letter but of the Spirit; for the letter kills, but the Spirit gives life. (2 Cor. 3:5–6)

Where our fleshly efforts cannot perfect us inwardly, the Spirit perfects us.

Are you so foolish? Having begun in the Spirit, are you now being made perfect by the flesh? . . . Therefore He who supplies the Spirit to you and works miracles among you, does He do it by the works of the law, or by the hearing of faith? (Gal. 3:3, 5)

The Spirit does for us what we cannot do on our own: he justifies and sanctifies.

He saved us, through the washing of regeneration and renewing of the Holy Spirit. (Titus 3:5)

The Spirit enables us to pursue righteousness and do all that God asks of his followers.

I say then: Walk in the Spirit, and you shall not fulfill the lust of the flesh. For the flesh lusts against the Spirit, and the Spirit against the flesh; and these are contrary to one another, so that you do not do the things that you wish. (Gal. 5:16–17)

The Holy Spirit, as is evident from even this small glimpse of Scripture, is the intimate, dynamic Person of the Godhead who is acting in and through us daily to live the Christian life. He is called our Counselor, our Advocate, our Intercessor, and our Helper. He seeks, saves, and sanctifies. He convicts of truth and sin and helps us to know the mind of God. The Holy Spirit is a living, breathing, affecting sticky note for the heart.

So let's stop pretending we can be good Christians according to how we behave or look or speak or make decisions. Our external behaviors often look really good on paper, but we all know that good Christian behaviors do nothing to create joy in our hearts or help us know God's love or enable us to fight off the lusts of the flesh. Let's give up on this idea that a list of behaviors is the way to the abundant life.

Let's also stop giving ourselves and others trite answers in the face of the daily struggles and realities of life. Directing people to have a quiet time, pray more, or go to church more isn't going to change anything at the heart level. Directing people to God himself for comfort, security, and the ability to face the most difficult of circumstances? That is when we invite the Holy Spirit to come alive in our hearts to mend, lead, convict, and comfort.

Let's stop fighting against what we all know from experience to be true: we can't live this Christian life. We need help. Let's fall into our weakness, not in a giving-up sense or a self-flogging sense, but in recognition that we live only by the power of God. "For though He was crucified in weakness, yet He lives by the power of God. For we also are weak in Him, but we shall live with Him by the power of God" (2 Cor. 13:4).

But just how do we live by the power of the Holy Spirit?

Ask for Help

I've been intrigued by that question in my own life as I've recognized my tendency to revert to the goodness gospel.

I find that when life gets busy, when demands are high, I put my head down and charge ahead. I white-knuckle it, gritting my teeth through it all, and I plot a finish line, a point ahead when I can lay down all responsibilities and rest. But then the finish line moves, and I want to quit it all. Unloading the dishwasher feels like moving a boulder up the hill, doing the laundry like running a marathon.

But something else happens when my head is down and I'm charging ahead: I miss out on life. I forget to look at the leaves changing and actually enjoy my favorite season. I bark at my children to clean up messes instead of really seeing my children and touching them. I fail to enjoy my days because I'm just trying to make it to bedtime. This is a joyless way to live.

In the carpool lane one morning, I thought about where I was and where I wanted to be and what's kept me from being there. I just didn't want to be a crazy person ruled by a to-do list. Very gently, God spoke into my heart: *You are fighting for joy, yes, but are you casting your cares upon me? Don't you know I want responsibility for your days?*

I had not been casting my cares upon him. They were bunched up heavy on my shoulders, and the weight was wearying me. I had been faithful to spend time in the Word, but I had not released my concerns to him. I hadn't asked for help. No wonder I just wanted to sit on the couch and stare at the television.

In reality, that's not what I want. I don't want to live like a zombie, white-knuckling my way through a maze of responsibilities. I don't want to be an unsafe person to myself. Most of all, I don't want to clog the power of God from moving in and through me.

I want to live by the power of God, fully alive to him and his grace to me.

To do this, I've realized, I can't revert to my innate tendencies of formula and forcing things. I must receive the help God offers me every day through the Holy Spirit. Because if the Spirit is the only One who can work in the inner man, if this is a place only he can reach, it seems it would be of utmost priority that I learn to ask for his help and to receive his help.

I hate asking for help. It breaks my little self-sufficient heart into pieces. But that's a very good thing because it's just that self-death that is necessary to receive from God and follow him.

In order to live the Christian life as God intends us to live it, we have to learn to ask for his help in everything, to rely on the power and wisdom of God rather than our own abilities or wisdom. This is difficult to do, often because we don't trust he will actually lead and convict us if we ask, or because we don't trust where he'll lead us. We *certainly* struggle to trust that he'll do it for others, so we boss people around way too much. We find security in control and in controlling the circumstances surrounding those we care most about. It's risky to admit our weakness and inability to bring life transformation; it's risky to trust a God we can't see and who often has very different ideas of how things should be than we do.

Some of us think of ourselves as competent for the Christian life, and we need to recognize the lie that we have something good to offer in and of ourselves. We need to learn the humble art of dependence.

The rest of us know we're not competent and need to recognize the truth that we are given help that makes us adequate. We need to learn to place our confidence in our Helper and leave the control and the production of results to him.

Relying on the Holy Spirit isn't loosey-goosey stuff. He is God, not a power to be manipulated according to our will and desires or for our emotional benefit. He is a Helper given by God; he is God himself helping us in our daily lives.

He knows what he's doing. We can rely on him.

I was reminded of just how much we can rely on him through my middle son.

"Is this the way home?" he piped up from the backseat, concern in his voice. We were on a stretch of road close to home, but one he evidently didn't recognize.

"Yes, of course it is, honey," I responded and turned back to the conversation I was having with my husband.

A few seconds later, he interrupted again. "Are we going home? Is this the way home?" In the front seat, we found this humorous, seeing as how we were literally a mile from home and on a road that we'd traveled multiple times, but we stifled our grins and tried to reassure him. "Yes, sweetie, this is the way home. I promise. We're very close. You'll see in just a second when we exit the highway."

But he simply would not let it go, turning his concern to the parent driving. "Dad, are you *sure* you know the way?" I glanced back at him to see he was sitting up straight, turning his head in every direction with true apprehension on his face, attempting to pinpoint his whereabouts.

My reassurances having failed, Kyle addressed him directly and at the very root of his apprehension: "Son, you're just going to have to trust that I know where we are, that I know where we're going, and that I know how to get us there."

With Kyle's words, my stifled grin turned to compassion. I also sometimes wonder where I am, where I'm going, and if the Person navigating really knows the way. I also feel apprehensive when the landmarks look unfamiliar and when a destination appears further away than it is in reality. Like my son, I also question and doubt over and over even though the ability of the Navigator has proven to be perfectly accurate. As I thought about these things, I laughed at myself. My concerns about the future and God's ability to produce spiritual fruit in my life are equally as silly as my son questioning our ability to drive him home.

Hearing Kyle's words to our son was like hearing God speak down deep in my heart: *Christine, you're just going to have to trust*

*that I know where you are, that I know where you're going, and that
I know how to get you there. You're going to have to rely on me.*
This is a truth I have to return to *every single day.* God is leading (and leading well), and I am to follow his leading. I must trust
that I don't have to figure things out on my own or decipher a code
to uncover what God wants for me, for my ministry, and for my
family. I don't have to force anything. I need to trust that he will
speak to me and lead me.

There is a reason why Scripture says there is freedom where
the Spirit is: we don't have to convict ourselves. We don't have to
worry that we won't know what God wants to say to us. We don't
have to come up with our own list of ways we should serve the
Lord. We don't have to freak out about controlling everything.
We don't have to remain stuck in sin or fear there isn't a way out
of it. We don't have to condemn ourselves. We have a Helper, the
Holy Spirit, who is responsible for conviction that leads to repentance (not condemnation), who helps us know the mind of God,
who shows us the way out of sin, and who leads us where God
wants us and empowers us for ministry when we're there. There
is profound peace and assurance in the Spirit, *if we will just look
to him to be our help.*

Recognizing His Lead

I've learned to recognize the Holy Spirit's leading in my life. I've
learned to acknowledge my lack of competency and ability apart
from God, to ask for his help—even if it's just a simple prayer of
acknowledgment and petition before going into a conversation—
and to wait by faith for his movement. Relying on the Holy Spirit's
help requires a whole lot of waiting, I've discovered. Sometimes
his help is an overwhelming nudge, and I could tell you incredible
stories of how he's led me and made his plans known to me. The

Holy Spirit's help in everyday life is not typically that overwhelming nudge but rather a simple little nudge; however, more often than not it comes through reading Scripture, praying, and journaling about what I've read.

For example, one morning as I opened my Bible, I was thinking about what a mom of teenagers and fellow pastor's wife had told me when I complained to her about how hard church planting was. She said, "It doesn't get any easier."

When she said it, I audibly groaned. You mean there is no magical day when parenting and ministry become comfortable, second nature, and obstacle-free?

Her words had exposed a false idea I had that I could work hard enough and long enough to control, plan, organize, and structure my life until it could be squeezed into a pretty little box, wrapped up so nice and neat. Tidy. Manageable. Perfect.

I know I can't do it. When I tape up one side, the other flops open. The contents of life are so big and unmanageable that I only frustrate myself when I think I can handle it all by myself—and yet sometimes I still try.

That's what I was thinking of as I opened my Bible to read in the Psalms.

And he came to me through his Word.

He didn't come to me in a gentle whisper as he so often does. He came like a warrior king, flooding my senses with an understanding of his power and might. *Who do you think you are?* He seemed to say. *I am the Creator God and I hold the whole universe together. You are broken and frail; you cannot.* He showed me how my efforts to control and structure my days were prideful and laughable. And then, as I was broken and bent, he gently lifted my head and invited me to come hide under the shadow of his wings. To quit trying to tie the nice, neat bow on top of life. To depend on him, the only one who *absolutely can* take care of things.

He flexed his power and might to me, not to show off or to berate me but rather so I'd see that he powerfully and mightily takes care of his children and so I'd depend on him.

This is but one example of how I've learned to recognize the Holy Spirit's leading through Scripture.

⟨⎯⎯⎯⎯⎯⟩

The Bible is specific about the role of the Spirit in the believer's life so we can be certain in our recognition of his movement and leading in our lives. Scripture is also clear that he always leads us in certain ways, down a certain path. As we walk in lockstep with him, we can be sure we are in God's protective shadow and are following his loving leadership. How do we recognize the Holy Spirit's movement? Where does he lead us?

He leads us to truth. Jesus said that when the Holy Spirit would come, he would convict of truth. The Holy Spirit tells us the truth about God and helps us to know and believe the truth that Jesus Christ is Lord. We can trust that it is the Holy Spirit who is leading us when he aligns our hearts with Scripture and convicts us of its truth. This conviction does not equal condemnation because those who walk in the Spirit are free from condemnation, but his conviction does lead to godly sorrow and repentance.[4] We can distinguish condemnation from conviction in that condemnation is general, accusatory, and leads to hopelessness. Conviction is specific, gently firm, and hopeful; conviction reminds us that the Holy Spirit will help us change.

He leads us to righteousness. The Holy Spirit convicts us of our need for righteousness and leads us to where that righteousness can be found: Jesus Christ. As he convinces us of both our need and our reception of imputed righteousness, we recognize a growing love and desire for obedience in our lives. He leads us away from the lusts of the flesh.[5]

He leads us to hope. The Holy Spirit gives us eyes to see what lies beyond the physical realm. For one thing, because he dwells in us as a guarantee of our future home, he gives us an eager antici-pation for our future righteousness.[6] And in our present state, he makes us adequate and competent to fulfill the Christian calling.

He leads us to serve others. The Holy Spirit will compel us to use the freedom we have in him as an opportunity to love others. Rather than focusing inward, we are compelled outward, to give and serve out of a longing for others to experience what we have experienced in Christ. He even gives us special gifts to help us love, serve, and edify others in the Church.

The Bible often speaks of the Holy Spirit in imagery: he is like water, wind, fire, or breath. These are difficult elements to contain and sometimes difficult to see, but they are all elements that show when they've been somewhere. Flood waters leave watermarks, wind bends trees, fire gives warmth and leaves ashes, and breath forms condensation on the window on cold winter mornings. If Scripture describes the Holy Spirit as being like these elements, we can be assured that he too will leave his mark on our lives as we invite him to move in and through us. Residuals of walking in the Spirit are love (toward God and others), freedom from sin, righteousness, life, and peace. We can know if we're walking and serving in the Spirit if we experience an increase of these residual marks in our lives.

The Spirit and Spiritual Disciplines

Knowing we have a Helper in the Holy Spirit gives us a fresh per-spective on spiritual disciplines—everything from Bible reading to prayer, fasting, giving, and church attendance.

As I was coming to recognize my goodness obsession, I didn't know quite how to view spiritual disciplines. For many years, I looked to spiritual disciplines as a checkpoint of how I was doing as a Christian. I was a "good" Christian if I did them and a "bad" one if I did not. But this to do list way of practicing spiritual dis ciplines, I discovered, is self-oriented. I created them. I set certain standards for myself, and I used them as a type of formula for spiritual maturity.

In this scenario, God was a supporting actor and I was both director and main actor. I could, in effect, practice spiritual disciplines without actually relating to God. Those disciplines in themselves could not change my heart or cause me to grow spiritually. In all my efforts to effect change in my life, something was missing.

That's because spiritual disciplines are not intended as *replacements* for the Holy Spirit. They are intended as ways to *ask for* and *receive* help from the Holy Spirit. God is the director and main actor. We belong to him. Spiritual disciplines, when practiced correctly, place us in positions of submission and acknowledgment of need, and help us be ready receptors when the Holy Spirit moves, leads, speaks, or convicts. I am essentially using spiritual disciplines like a door, opening my heart to God, ready to receive from him. They are a means of continual receiving and, therefore, are vitally important.

Knowing the role of the Holy Spirit actually elevates the spiritual disciplines beyond a to-do list, because they are our way of asking for the Holy Spirit's help.

Prayer, for example, becomes a vital connection to God. If, as we've established, the Holy Spirit is the only One who can reach into the heart of man and if, as we've established, we can't control or affect heart transformation, our role and responsibility in partnership with the Holy Spirit is to pray for him to act.

For me, this comes into play often as I consider how to help my children know God and trust in him. When my first son was born, a struggle with fear was also born in my heart. In the beginning trivial fears gripped me: What if he won't sleep when the book says he should sleep? What if he cries like this for the rest of his life? What if I never shower again? But when he was diagnosed as having autism, the realities of motherhood and the weight of profound fears landed hard. Would he ever speak? Was his future a hopeful one? Would he ever enjoy relationships? Would I be able to parent this child how he needed to be parented?

What I soon realized was that all moms struggle with fear at some level. Every mother wants her child's emotional, physical, and spiritual well-being, and every mother wants to do right by her child. Every mother fears that she might not be enough, or that life might be a big bully to the one she loves.

I recognize my fears as a mother, and I also recognize my typical responses to those fears. I either anxiously feed the fear and am motivated by it, or I attempt to tamp down the fear through my own effort.

My primary method of handling fear is the second response—to control fear through effort. And what do I fear most? I fear my children won't know and be assured of what God has done for them in Christ. I fear that they won't love God or love others well. So I set goals of what I want to instill into my children. I make lists of activities to help them grow. I write down ideas that other mothers share. I scour blogs and Pinterest. I pack the schedule with opportunities. I help them pursue friendships. I peel open the Bible every morning after breakfast and read it to them.

This doesn't sound so bad, so why is this response to fear such a bad thing? Being purposeful with my children is not inherently bad, but *if it is motivated by fear, it is sin.*[7] It's sin because, if we believe that our efforts are the way to protect our children or produce heart and character transformation in them, we're saying that we are God. We're saying we can control life and circumstances. We're saying we have the power to do what only God can do. *This is why controlling our fears through effort is so dangerous.*

I've been thinking a lot lately about my typical responses to fear as a mother and recognizing that, truly, my children belong to

God and I have no ability to produce character in them. I can teach them and lead them toward this end, but *only God can actually do it*. Wouldn't I much rather allow him to protect, provide for, and work in the hearts of my kids? A million times, yes.

So what is our response to the fears we have as mothers—and in any area of life, for that matter? God gives us a way to ask for help and for things to change: we can pray! We are to pray fervently for our children and ask the Holy Spirit to do what only he can do. And we not only pray, but we trust the answer he will give, which is so often different than what we think it will be or should be.

We must also be obedient to put the structure in place that he asks us to put in place in our families, but we recognize it is not actually this structure that will do anything. It's him, and it's only ever been him.

This is true for anything we are concerned about, whether it's marriage, career, ministry, relationships, or suffering. The change or growth we desire can only be done by the Spirit. So instead of controlling, we pray. Instead of being self-sufficient, we pray. Instead of trusting in behavior modification, we pray. Instead of being afraid, we pray.

We have a Helper, after all, who Jesus promised would help us when we call on him.

This is, in fact, the posture of a child who looks with complete security and assurance to her father for help and guidance. We are now children, brought to the Father's table, and, because we are no longer orphans, we don't have to act as orphans who must take care of themselves. Jesus said, "I will not leave you orphans; I will come to you" (John 14:18). How did he come to us? Through the indwelling of the Holy Spirit. The Holy Spirit is our guide and our sufficiency, and by depending on him we are looking to our Father for help and for our needs to be met each day. The Holy Spirit leads us to the Father-heart of God.

For as many as are led by the Spirit of God, these are sons of God. For you did not receive the spirit of bondage again to fear, but you received the Spirit of adoption by whom we cry out, "Abba, Father." The Spirit Himself bears witness with our spirit that we are children of God, and if children, then heirs—heirs of God and joint heirs with Christ (Rom. 8:14–17).

Obedience: Following His Lead

We learn to recognize the Holy Spirit's leading and we open the door to hear the Spirit's leading through spiritual disciplines, but we have another responsibility, and that is to obey when he leads. It's not enough to receive the Holy Spirit's conviction, direction, counsel, and leadership; we must then fall in step with him by following and obeying. This is what Paul meant when he said, "If we live in the Spirit, let us also walk in the Spirit" (Gal. 5:25).

This is where it gets good! When we listen for the Spirit's leading through the practice of spiritual disciplines and when we choose to submit ourselves to him through obedience, our lives are transformed by God and we are freed to love and serve others by the power of the Spirit.

The Holy Spirit may lead you in some exciting ways. He may open doors and relationships to you that give you great opportunities to share the gospel and impact lives.

Or he may not. He may ask you to continue doing what you're doing, even if it's unseen faithfulness he's asking for.

The reason we obey is to please the God who loves us. The results are up to him; they're his concern, not ours.

I've learned this most through church planting and parenting.

When people ask if we're going to have more children, I always say that our church is our fourth child. We birthed it when our sons were five years, two years, and six months old, respectively, and it really did feel like we delivered another child. A tiring, up-all-night kind of child.

Everyone told us we would feel this way, that planting a church was like giving birth to a baby, but hardly anyone told us that the baby would have to grow up and that we would be the ones to see it through the sleepless nights, the terrible twos, and the perils of puberty. Our fourth child is only six, so we don't know about puberty yet, although we've experienced a transition that has felt awkward and emotional so perhaps we're proudly now a tween.

When we birthed this church, no one told us to focus more on the parenting than the birth, and I was taken aback by the extent of the work. I figured one or two years max and we'd be off to the races, enjoying the fruit of our labor, reveling in a fully formed church. A two-year-old can barely talk, however, and she is likely not potty-trained. I know that's a weird analogy to use regarding the church, but it gives a picture of the messiness and the grueling work involved. There was a point when it hit me: *this child has to be raised and that's going to take years.* Church planting is a long haul, and there's no way around that.

In a church plant, everything starts from the ground up. Like those of a child, each new stage of development is a new start, with its own fresh challenges and unique needs. I admit this is disheartening at times. A few Sundays ago, I looked around at our church and huffed at God, "This isn't what I imagined it would be when I signed on the dotted line with you." I hadn't imagined it would be such an extensive commitment, and I hadn't imagined the church makeup we currently had. The Lord quickly responded, clearly and firmly: *Yes, but this is the church I have built.*

I knew what he was saying, and it stung in a good way. Church planting isn't about me; it never has been and never will be. God will not work around my idea of what our church should be, which is oftentimes centered on my own comfort and desires. I've experienced this same humbling in parenting. The children God has given me are so different than what I imagined, but isn't this his good plan? The questions, then, are not, "How will they reflect on me?" or "How will they serve me?" but simply "Will I be faithful to shepherd them well?"

I knew what else he was reminding me of: this church hasn't been our doing. Just as with our physical children, we gave birth to something God knit together, and we are stewards of the gospel as we raise this church-child God has given us. Yes, there were a precious few in the delivery room who have been with this child since the beginning, and, yes, this means we care about this baby more than anyone else. *But it is not ours. We are but stewards.*

Am I willing not only to birth a real child or a church-child but to do the hard work of raising those children? There's nothing cool about that, nothing that will make me a Christian celebrity or Mom of the Year. But relying on the Holy Spirit, obeying his leading, and trusting him with the results are what enable me to scream forth a baby in the delivery room and raise that baby into a fully functioning mature adult.

God's job is life transformation and salvation and spiritual growth. My job is faithfulness and obedience.

Received from Start to Finish

As we talk about obedience, we must stop again and recall what's already been said: in and of ourselves, we aren't able to do it. We cannot be good, and to try to be good is the old life when we were alive to the law and alive to self-sufficiency.

Without this reminder ever in front of us, we're prone to return to striving for goodness and creating external structures to keep ourselves in line. In fact, our self-imposed religious regulations only increase sin, condemnation, and frustration.

Our goal is to respond to God's leadership.

As we give ourselves to the Spirit, follow his leading, and ask him for the help we need to obey his leading, we don't have to worry about keeping ourselves in line. *We can trust him.* He always leads us away from the lusts of our flesh and, by the Spirit, enables us to go against what our flesh wishes to do.

We can either give ourselves to our flesh, which is sin, or we can give ourselves to God, which leads to righteousness and peace. I'm not talking about salvation. I'm talking about the daily life of the believer.

> Therefore do not let sin reign in your mortal body, that you should obey it in its lusts. And do not present your members as instruments of unrighteousness to sin, but present yourselves to God as being alive from the dead, and your members as instruments of righteousness to God. (Rom. 6:12–13)

He who makes us alive to God and helps us fulfill this is the Holy Spirit. We simply have to receive the help he offers.

We receive God's love and the help he gives us in the Holy Spirit together; they can't be separated. Knowing God's love motivates us to obey the Spirit's leading because we want to love him back, and we recognize that willing submission to him is how we do so. As we look at the ocean of love in his eyes, we naturally trust that his heart is for us, and that what he asks of us is for his honor and our joy. And so we want to obey.

The Christian life is received from start to finish.

What is there left to say, really?

God has taken responsibility for everything in our past, present, and future: salvation (past and future), a source for helping us live to God (present), a complete removal of condemnation (past, present, and future), adoption as children (past, present, and future), and a hope greater than any present circumstance (present and future).

It's summed up like this: God is for us!

And because God is for us, who can stand against us? Nothing, not even death's sting, can come in and remove God's favor. Because God's way has nothing to do with what we can or can't do or what we do or don't do, and because it has everything to do with what Christ has done and what the Spirit continues to do in us, we can't ever be separated from his great love.

He gives more than enough, so that we are more than conquerors.

We simply receive what he so freely offers.

And we rejoice!

6

Receiving His Freedom

I DROVE BY THE HIGH SCHOOL near our house on Friday night during their football game and marveled at how few people were in the stands. With the band playing and the cool fall evening settling down into darkness, I recalled my own high school days in a state where everyone's out at the stadium for Friday night lights and football reigns.

I felt homesick.

My dad called, his East Texas accent glaringly obvious to my newly acquired East Coast ears. I mentioned it, laughing, and he commented that my accent, my sound of home, was completely gone. Kyle says there are some words where I twang, but only some, and this makes me surprisingly sad, a bit like feeling homesick.

I go to Texas, though, and it's still home yet it's also foreign now. I notice every woman wears makeup and most wear large jewelry and everyone gets all dolled up, as they say. The men drive trucks and people look you in the eye. And the billboards and chain restaurants? Were they there in this quantity before?

There are megachurches on every corner, and when I tell my Texas friends that people where I live don't have a category for these buildings and these programs, they look at me a little funny. And then their eyes fill with far-off wonder when I speak of snow and autumn and mountains and how beautiful it is in Charlottesville.

That is home for me now: Charlottesville, Virginia, the place of four seasons, mountains, Subarus, bumper stickers, lacrosse, bow ties, Thomas Jefferson, and the place of no Tex-Mex, no Friday night lights, no George Bush Parkways, no bluebonnets, and no nine-month summers.

That feels right and wrong all at the same time, like I'm a little bit homesick whether I'm in Texas or Virginia. But for what am I homesick? Comfort? Familiarity? A cultural identity?

I've realized I often define home (and myself) according to cities and states, and that I've been trying to figure out where my home is for years now. We visit family in beloved Texas and it only feels 75 percent like home (100 percent while scarfing down queso at a Tex-Mex restaurant), but in Virginia, a place that we love and where we've built a great life, there is still a small part of me that doesn't feel it's home. *Where is home?*

Our True Home

This really can be a question more about my comfort and identity than anything else. It drives me, this desire to call a place home, to not feel half-home in two different places. I look at my friends who have gone East from the West or West from the East, and I wonder if they know where their home is and if they feel like this too. It seems silly to say, but it feels like a sacrifice to be half-at-home all the time, to raise my children in a culture different than the one

I grew up in, and to have become a little bit Texas and a little bit East Coast but not fully either one.

You can imagine how delighted (and convicted) I was, then, to read this:

> Therefore Jesus also, that He might sanctify the people with His own blood, suffered outside the gate. Therefore let us go forth to Him, outside the camp, bearing His reproach. *For here we have no continuing city, but we seek the one to come.* (Heb. 13:12–14, emphasis added)

As a Christian, I identify myself with Jesus, who the Bible says had no certain place to lay his head at night. He embraced the isolation of going outside the gate, because he knew his greater purpose. He didn't belong to a specific group of people. In fact, the one group of people he could have most closely identified with, according to his family or birthplace, rejected him.

He went outside the gate, outside the camp. He went to die so grace might live.

If I identify with him, what does that say about my home? It means that no city or state or house is my home. It means that my longing for familiarity and my desire for home will never be satisfied in Texas or Virginia or anywhere else I may live in my life. It means that as long as I am on earth, *Christ himself is my home.* I am to identify with him more than I am a physical earthly place.

We identify ourselves with many good but lesser things: culture, race, relationships, vocation, nationality, and religious tradition. We joke about our loyalties in college football and huddle with those who make similar lifestyle choices. These identities make us who we are and inform our lives.

But then there are the thoughts and experiences that shape our identity that we rarely name out loud because we feel we're the only one: bitterness, woundedness, shame, fear, doubt, anger, hatred,

loneliness, insecurity, competitiveness, jealousy. We wouldn't intro-
duce ourselves to new acquaintances using these labels, but we think
them: *Hello. I'm completely unlikeable*, or *Hi. I have done things
that, if you knew, you would never speak to me again.*

These are, if we're honest, our true identity markers. We think
them, recite them to ourselves, and ruminate in them on our worst
days and in our most difficult moments. It seems hopeless and
impossible that we'll ever be free of them. They are as familiar to
us as our homes and our oldest friends.

We dwell in these thoughts. But despite their familiarity, they
are not true friends and are not at all our true reality.

Our true home is Christ, and this home is formed and sustained
by the bricks and mortar of grace. We've entered by repentance
and faith, made possible by his grace, and now we dwell in and
breathe and are invaded by him, a gift of grace.

In the context of the Hebrews passage, the call to a Jew to
go outside the gate with Christ would have been shocking and
disgraceful because it would have meant essentially abandoning
everything: their Jewish identity, their Jewish community, and their
Jewish practices.

Our call to go forth to Christ is to take on Christ and abandon
everything that is not identified with him. We abandon our old
ways. We abandon our old self. We abandon any notion of reaching him according to man-made gospels, including the goodness
gospel. We abandon our personal ambitions, goals, and agendas
in order to take his own.

But we also must abandon what Christ, in his grace, has forgiven
and removed. We abandon bitterness, foreclose on fear, and leave
shame forever. Only grace can do that.

So our call to go outside the gate and dwell in Christ, making him
our home, is a call to freedom. We are freed from the gated confines
of the old life, with its rules and regulations and its unfettered sin.
We are freed from the power of unforgiveness and from trying to

please everyone all the time. We are free to make our home in the gospel, to breathe its air and feel its pulse in our veins.

To make our home in the gospel, we must abandon all else, all other dwellings, and receive grace.

Dynamite Grace

The gospel—Christ—is synonymous with grace. When we talk about our dwelling place, our home, we're talking about grace. We entered by the grace of Christ, we remain because of the grace of Christ, and our future salvation and hope are because of the grace of Christ. We live inside grace. This is where we've gone outside the gate to dwell. This is what we've received and continue to receive.

Grace isn't this sugary-sweet concept that we apply like a Band-Aid to our failures. There is a reason we sing that grace is amazing: the grace of God as shown in Christ is tangible and real and has power like dynamite to release the shackles of so many of our hang-ups, so many of the things that usually send us right back onto the treadmill of chasing our own goodness.

Grace is a powerful shield, an explosive force against the philosophies and the worldly wisdom of man and the wily schemes of spiritual beasts. Grace touches the deepest parts of us, changing how we treat our physical bodies, what we think and feel, what we do and how we do it, and how we respond to people around us. It is the power that sets and keeps the prisoner free. It is the salve to the deepest wounds a person can suffer. It is Christ himself standing between us and anything that is not of him.

Grace makes us free and keeps us free. As we receive God's love, the power of his Spirit to live this life, and his grace, we receive our freedom and we're invited to remain free.

That's just it: we can know we're living in the gospel if we're walking in freedom. We live free from sin and any power it could hold or has held over us, because we are no longer slaves to sin. We can choose obedience and to flee from temptation. We live free from the dread of death because our home in grace cannot ever be taken away, whether in life or by physical death. We live freed from the law; perfectionism is no longer breathing down our necks or clawing at our hearts, because Christ redeemed us from the curse of the law, having become a curse for us.

What freedom! Don't you see it? No circumstance, difficulty, sin, or trial can destroy us if Christ has even overcome our greatest enemy and greatest fear—death. Not only did he overcome it, but he parades death, Satan, and sin around in humiliation and defeat like a victor bringing the prisoners and their spoils back from war.[1] We don't have to walk around defeated, as if *we* are the prisoners. *We* don't dwell in shackles. We dwell in grace and the freedom he's won for us.

But what exactly is that freedom? What exactly have we been freed *from*? What have we left behind as we've received our new reality of redemption, as we've identified ourselves with Christ?

Grace Frees Us from Ourselves

This morning I woke up with a restless heart. It's par for the course these days, as I sense God stripping away significant roles I've relied on for my sense of purpose, direction, and effectiveness in ministry. I gave them up willingly, knowing God was asking them of me, but now that the rubber is meeting the road, as they say, I feel uncomfortable and unsettled.

Who am I without these roles? That's the question roiling below the surface of my discomfort. It goes further: How do I prove my worth when there aren't opportunities to perform? How do I measure my impact in ministry when I feel like I'm not really doing anything, when God is simply asking for faith and trust in the midst of my unsettledness? What do I have to show for myself in this season of life?

In reality, although I fight and flail against it, I recognize his gracious hand. I see that he's stripping away some unhealthy patterns of thought and action. There is the pride issue, for one, and the lurking fleshly desire for honor. There is the spiritual performance and production issue that drives me toward the law rather than toward grace. And it's quite clear to me that God has asked me to release these things to make way for something else. Something I can't quite see yet. Something he lovingly keeps from me as he purges the sin from my heart.

This doesn't feel good. I find myself seeking encouragement from people and trying to finagle a way out of the discomfort I'm sitting in. Through eyes of faith, however, I recognize God is prying my hands off of self and proclaiming the profound joy and satisfaction of dwelling in him.

He's proclaiming that to me through the gospel. And there is freedom in it.

I haven't gone to the Word with great enthusiasm in these days of uncertainty because I much prefer a quick fix, which is, of course, something that would feed the "self" begging to burst to the front of the line. But nevertheless I've gone to the Word and let it do its work in me.

Returning to the gospel reminds me of the futility of vain pursuits, the exaltation of self being prime among them. I am free to gaze on the beauty and depth of God and his mercy rather than obsessing about myself.

The gospel ransoms me from my prison of performance. *In Christ, I am not my performance.* This is perhaps the first and most important freedom I've received in Christ. Grace frees me from a focus on self and all the sins and burdens that come along with it: selfishness, insecurity, pride, trying to prove myself worthy, seeking love and approval, fear of not being enough.

Like a giant wave, the gospel rises above this petty focus on self, crushing every facet of our selfishness and self-centeredness. We no longer need to seek our own honor and worth because we are loved by Love himself. His love is greater. His grace is greater. His approval is sure. We cannot add or take away from that love and, therefore, though we may feel unsettled, our souls are eternally at rest.

This is the explosive power of the gospel: it frees us from ourselves and enables us to live for God and for the sake of others. As we see our sin compared with the holiness of God, and as we see grace applied to that chasm, it's humbling and awe-inspiring. Life becomes no longer about us and our prideful pursuits.

Tim Keller calls this freedom the freedom of self-forgetfulness.

> Every single day we are on trial. That is the way that everyone's identity works. In the courtroom, you have the prosecution and the defence. And everything we do is providing evidence for the prosecution or evidence for the defence. Some days we feel we are winning the trial and other days we feel we are losing it. But Paul says [in 1 Corinthians 4:3–4] that he has found the secret. The trial is over for him. He is out of the courtroom. It is gone. It is over. Because the *ultimate* verdict is in.
>
> Do you realize it is only in the gospel of Jesus Christ that you get the verdict before the performance? The atheist might say that they get their self-image from being a good person. They are a good person and hope that eventually they will get a verdict that confirms they are a good person. Performance leads to the verdict. . . . But Paul is saying that in Christianity the verdict leads to performance. . . . In Christianity, the moment we believe, God imputes Christ's perfect performance to us as if it were our own, and adopts us into his family. In other words, God can say to us just as he once said to Christ, "You are My Son, whom I love; with you I am well pleased."[2]

Grace Frees Us from the Fear of Man

When we aren't gazing at God's mercy and letting it soak us like a fresh spring rain, we become a self-focused ball of insecurities. When we're self-focused and insecure, our measuring stick quickly becomes the response of others. *Do they like us? Do they think we're on the right track? Do they approve of how we live?*

Before we made our home in the gospel, we were enslaved to the law. If we continue to live enslaved to the law though followers of Jesus, we develop a certain perverted gospel called legalism, or following man-made rules, and this kind of legalism has profound consequences.

One such consequence is that we assent with our mouths to being followers of God but in reality we are followers of man. We are people-pleasers. We are people-impressers. We are also people-judgers.

We tend to become entangled in a constant desire to please others. If what we do outwardly is only for the benefit of others so they will view us as "good" Christians, then we can be sure we are missing what God is saying to us and asking us to do.

The more we fear God and what he thinks, the less it matters what others think and say about us.

It's almost unexplainable, the sense of satiation and completeness that invades the heart when our eyes are fixed on the cross. At the cross of Christ, God declares not only that we are forgiven, but that we are family. He calls us children, *beloved* children. There is a tenderness and an enduring love that characterize our Father God.

I know when I am not fixed on this grace because then I am obsessed with what others think of me, and my estimation is that they look at me with condemnation.

I know, in fixing my eyes on others, that I am turning from

the ocean of approval and belonging found in Christ to a puddle of imperfect love found in people. But sometimes the approval of others drives me, and it drives me right into anxiety, fear, and self-sufficiency.

As I read the Word, however, in an almost tangible way God puts his hand to my face and lifts my chin to look at his grace. And then I am at rest again. It is well with my soul.

We must get this right, we must look to his grace toward us, because there is a second part of this, another side to the people-pleasing coin, and it's this: the more we know what God wants *for* us, the less it matters what others want *from* us.

Too many times, we don't see grace in God's heart and so we don't go to him for the approval and love he offers freely. We are blind because we don't know the very heart of his gospel.

When we grasp grace, or at least attempt to grab hold of the ocean, we recognize that our focus has often wrongly been on what we think God wants *from* us. He wants our service. He wants our holiness. So we try and try again.

But grace shows us God's heart, and what we see is that his heart is *for* us, and that he wants the best *for* us, and that everything flows from this heart.

If God is *for* us, who can be against us? If God is *for* us, we only want to be *for* him; we only want to rise to be who he created us to be.

The more we know what God wants *for* us, the less it matters what others want *from* us.

Every single day, we must turn to look at the cross and remember what was done there for us. We don't just remember the agony, but we look at what Christ accomplished for us. He opened the door of the Holy of Holies and introduced us into an intimate relationship with the Father God who loves us perfectly.

So the only way to freedom is to swim in grace's ocean and to know the heart from where it flows.

Grace Frees Us from Comparison and Competition

One spring, I opened my home on a weekly basis to a group of new moms to discuss biblical motherhood. Each of them arrived with their babies and baby gear in tow, as well as a palpable fear that they were getting it all wrong.

There is an inherent danger in gathering moms in a room: we immediately compare notes regarding our children's milestones, personalities, and sleep habits. Really, though, we are comparing ourselves, wondering if we are good moms and if our children reflect well on us.

When I had my first baby, I wanted to be a good mom. All moms want this, and, if we're not looking to grace, we look around at other moms and other children to measure ourselves. This is an exhausting and pressurized situation for all involved, including our children.

But this is not the way of grace, which I learned through brokenness and much repentance before God. God used his grace to till the hard ground of my heart, thoughts, and habits. He taught me to offer grace to others just as he had offered grace to me. I had to apologize to people and deal with the sin I had allowed into my life.

Comparison and competition, as I learned the hard way, are *not okay for God's children*, because they don't reflect his heart. Comparison and competition are sinful attitudes that result in sinful behaviors. They announce that we're orphans who don't have a loving Father to provide perfectly for our every need, or that he is a Father who doesn't love all of his children. When we compare and compete, we tell lies about our Father and we turn outsiders away from the gospel.

The only way we can kill our tendency for comparison and competition is to receive God's grace and understand that it's for everyone who is in Christ Jesus. We are all on a level playing field, although God often chooses to use people and their gifts differently. A heart of grace understands this. A heart of grace is able to cheer for others, rejoice in their victories, and pray for their good. A heart of grace trusts God enough to not have to fight to be seen or heard or understood or acknowledged. A heart of grace knows her identity, approval, and very beating come from him.

He is enough, so she is enough. He gives enough, so she has enough.

Grace frees us from the condemnation, guilt, and insecurities that divide people and kill relationships. When we understand what we've been given in Christ and *that he gives the same freely to others who call him Lord*, we recognize we are the same as others. We don't have to compete or compare. We don't need the approval of others or to live according to their directives. We don't have to judge or hold grudges.

We can live in grace and offer that same grace to others.

That's why, with these young moms, I addressed this tendency toward comparison on the first day. Until we stop comparing ourselves or telling other moms they should mother our way, I said, we will leave our time together feeling isolated and condemned.

The gospel of Christ, after all, holds no place for comparison. We are all equally in need of grace, and we all equally receive it as a gift from God. In regards to mothering, the gospel clearly applies.

None of us are good enough mothers.

Through Christ, God offers us grace in our mothering. He takes our meager efforts and produces spiritual fruit in us and our children. He is enough.

He has given us principles in Scripture as a framework for mothering.

He has also given us the Holy Spirit to *individually* lead and guide us in mothering our *unique* children.

What does this mean in day in, day out motherhood? It means we are all mothering toward the same goal—that our children know and worship God—but our methods for reaching that goal may vary

according to our unique families and circumstances, and, most im
portantly, according to the leadership of the Holy Spirit. Will he lead
every believer toward the same goal? Yes. Will he lead every believer
to that goal in the same way? No. And this is a *very good thing*.

In *The Fruit of Her Hands,* Nancy Wilson says, "Because every
family is a distinct cultural unit, it is good that our methods differ.
God did not intend for us to walk in lockstep with one another. We
ought to rejoice in a common commitment to biblical principles
and in the variety of methods God's people employ."[3]

Because of the gospel, then, the Mommy Wars have no place
among believers. After all, at the heart of the Mommy Wars are
pride ("I am more spiritual than that mother because I employ this
method and she does not"), competition ("My children are better
than hers because I employ this method"), and self-condemnation
("I am not spiritual enough or a good enough mother because I
don't employ the method that she does").

To end the Mommy Wars in the Church, we must learn to apply
the gospel not only to our own mothering but also to the mothering
methods of others. When we know God's grace, we stop looking
for validation from others for our methods and we are able to
extend grace to others; we celebrate and respect the different gifts
and styles of mothering as we move toward a common goal.

These are all the things I said to the new moms in my living room.
I pleaded with them so earnestly to remember grace, to turn off
the chorus of (good) voices on the internet and the (good) books
on their shelves, and to listen for and focus on the only voice that
matters, the quiet whisper of grace in Christ's voice.

Grace Frees Us from Fear

Fear lies at the foundation of our tendencies toward self-focus and
others-focus.

123

When we are self-focused, the fear is actually of God himself. We fear that we aren't enough in his presence or that we aren't living this life he's given with enough faith and purpose or that we aren't, well, enough. We feel we're a disappointment to him or that his wrath is hovering over us, so we live life in a state of panic. We're afraid to approach him, and this talk of communing with him at the table of grace is so very foreign that we can't even give it a second thought.

I know this fear very well. I lived in it for many years, driven by my conjured self-condemnation and guilt. It's taken different forms: fear of failing at being a mom to the kids he's given, fear of mediocrity in the calling he's given, fear of his impatience with my imperfection, fear of living a life that didn't make an impact.

One night I lay awake thinking about my fear, and I thought about a time in college when I worked at a summer camp.

As part of our preparation for campers, we learned to hold the safety ropes on the treetop activities, which culminated in the Pamper Pole. The Pamper Pole was a telephone pole covered in small pegs for climbing. We strapped each person attempting the Pamper Pole into a harness that was attached to a bungee cord. The bungee cord ensured that the climber wouldn't fall to the ground even if they fell off the pole. They'd end up dangling in the air right next to the pole with a look of sheer terror on their face, but they were *always* safe, whether they felt it or not.

That summer I watched as campers and even fellow counselors shimmied up the pole and then stopped in panic at the top, clinging and uncertain. Finally, with encouragement, they would step up on top of the pole and fling themselves toward the acrobat's bar hanging in front of it.

From the ground, this didn't appear too difficult, and I wondered why so many were frightened by it. But when it was my turn and I got to the top, to the part where I had nothing left to hold on to as I attempted to stand up, where the ground seemed dangerously far away, and where I struggled to trust that the harness would hold me if I fell, I understood why the Pamper Pole was named after a brand of diapers.

As I laid awake thinking about all the things I feared, especially the fear of not being enough, that feeling of ascending the Pamper Pole is what came to mind. The terror, the lack of trust, the overwhelming feeling of being on my own—all the same things that my fear speaks to me.

And then I remembered the harness. The fear of balancing myself on a tiny telephone pole swaying in the wind was (very) real. *But all along, whether I felt it or not, I had the harness on.*

Is this not the gospel? We *aren't* enough for God. We are deceived when we think we are enough *and* when we think we have to be enough. However, the fact that we aren't enough is only half of the equation. It's like an incomplete sentence, with the most important part left off.

We aren't enough, but God has made us enough by his grace.

When we worry that we aren't enough, it is the unnecessary fear, the fake fear of climbing the Pamper Pole and feeling we are on our own to make ourselves enough for God when all along we are locked into safety. Like the harness, God keeps us.

Thankfully, in grace, God frees us from fear. And he doesn't just free us; he authoritatively drives it away.

The book of Hebrews speaks well to this, reminding us of the extent Christ has gone to free us from our sin and the fear that we aren't enough before him. Hebrews says that Christ humbled himself by becoming a limited man so he could endure God's wrath in our place. God fulfilled the promise he made in an oath to Abraham so we might know how sure and steadfast our hope is. Christ was made our forever and unchangeable Priest so that he could save us to the *uttermost*. And Jesus, through his blood, made a way for us to enter into the Holy of Holies and to cleanse our consciences from dead works. After all that, the writer of Hebrews pleads with us to understand:

> Therefore, brethren, having boldness to enter the Holiest by the blood of Jesus, by a new and living way which He consecrated for us, through the veil, that is, His flesh, and having a High Priest over the house of God, let us draw near with a true heart in *full assurance* of faith. (Heb. 10:19–22, emphasis added)

Let us be people confident in what God has done for us! This confidence has nothing to do with us or what we have or have not done. This confidence is outside of us and on Christ, who has convincingly driven away condemnation, sin, guilt, division between us and God, and God's just wrath toward sin. Nothing stands in the way anymore between us and God. Therefore, we have nothing to fear.

Fear doesn't just arise from internal turmoil, however. It also arises around external circumstances. We fear what has happened in the past will happen again, we fear what may happen in the future, and we fear everything in between. But we don't have to cling to what we love in life, hold it tight to our chests, and hope for the best. Grace teaches us to seek security and peace in our unchanging God. Grace teaches us to fully and completely identify with Christ and to dwell in him.

When we recognize grace as a gift, we recognize everything in life—summit or valley, easy or difficult, certain or uncertain—is a residual gift of the first grace we received. We look to the Grace-Giver and *trust his heart for us*. We know our hope is in him, not in what he gives and takes away. This is a difficult part of grace and faith, and it can only be lived out through a deep understanding of Christ's grace.

Receiving Our Freedom

This, in essence, is what it means to live by grace: living with eyes wide open but boldly gazing on Christ. If the old life before Christ is a life of doing, pursuing, taking, modifying, or apathy leading to death, then the new life in Christ must look different than that. The old life is a life enslaved to sin and the deadness of soul. This old home seems familiar sometimes, because we live in a world where the old life reigns. But grace is no longer grace if we try to mix it with anything. We can't mix two different homes, two different identities, and two different pursuits. If so, the gospel becomes defiled and shattered, and our old home that we think we're homesick for enslaves us again. That's why we can confidently say that if we aren't experiencing and living in freedom from unrepentant sin, self, fear of man, and fear itself, it's likely we're not dwelling in the grace that Jesus won us on the cross.

The new life, then, is dead to our old ways and alive to God, alive to the joys of righteousness. In the new life, grace reigns. In our new life, we're not making our home in our accomplishments or in our popularity or in circumstances or in anything that changes. As Paul writes, we're not living as the self-sufficient do: in bondage, in debt to the law, and estranged from Christ. We're profiting from Christ by receiving the freedom and intimacy he offers. We're making our home in grace. We're clinging to it because it's all we have, and because we believe wholeheartedly that it's all we need.

Living alive to God has little to do with behavioral change and rote spiritual disciplines but rather with what happens deep in the soul. In other words, living alive to God is something only he can produce in me, because grace is a gift meant to be received with gratefulness and joy. So he makes me alive at salvation, and he makes me continually alive in sanctification, and I allow his grace to reign in my heart daily. I receive my freedom as I would a gift.

Normally when I think of gaining freedom, I think of charging forward in battle or fighting to be released from ties that bind me. But this is a freedom that has already been won for us. We simply walk by faith out of the open jail cell and *rest* in what has been given.

Remaining free is difficult. Temptation, worldly philosophy, and our very own flesh call us back to our captivity. That's precisely why Paul exhorts us to stand firm in the freedom for which Christ has made us free. But how do we do this? How do we stand firm in the freedom Christ has made available for us?

Because we are freed from sin's power, we grieve and repent over sin but also understand, receive, and are grateful for Christ's forgiveness. We refuse to condemn ourselves over failures and sin because Christ has removed the shackles of condemnation. Grace is overpowering and wild and free, and we choose daily to swim in its deepest ocean and revel in its depths. We cannot reach its end, and this says everything about God. That's the focus in freedom: not on our sin but on the grace and the Grace-Giver who has removed our sin.

Because we are freed from self-focus and we are not our performance, we boast in the cross alone. Just as we refuse to dwell on our past failures, we refuse to condemn ourselves for our weakness and inability to be perfect. We know that perfectionism and the comparison, pride, self-condemnation, isolation, and competition it births are heavy shackles. We put no confidence in our flesh because this is man's deadly way. Instead we boast in the perfection won for us by Christ on the cross. We rely on the Spirit for our competency, because where the Spirit is, there is freedom.

Because we are freed from the fear of man, we make it our aim, our heartbeat, our every goal, to please God. We refuse to live for the weak and finicky applause of man, because man's approval is no match for the unchanging love and approval God pours out onto his own. We are free from the labels and identities the world craves to place on us. Instead of living alive to the ever-changing "shoulds" of man, we live alive to his presence, his pleasure, his delight in us. We long to obey him because we love to experience the joy, the satisfaction, and, of course, the freedom of his blessing.

Because we are freed from fear and our hope is in a new kingdom
while still on earth, we value the expressions of that kingdom: faith,
grace, righteousness, love, and joyful obedience. Outside the gate,
where we identify with Christ, we find that the successful and victorious Christian life is measured not in dutiful outward expressions
but in inward expressions from a willing and submissive heart that
often lead to response. We recognize that duty and obligation are
chains around our heart but true freedom is experienced in deeper
faith, fuller hope, and greater love of God and man. "For in Christ
Jesus neither circumcision nor uncircumcision avails anything, but
faith working through love" (Gal. 5:6). Our value of these inward
expressions spills forth onto others—we value and encourage these
expressions in others as well, because just as they are our freedom
expressed, these values are their freedom as well.

This is our manifesto of freedom: we *will* dwell in the grace of
Christ. We will *never* return to our former home. We will *not* be
identified by bitterness or shame or anything other than Christ.

By planting my feet firmly in Christ, I am receiving from him
my reservation for future grace, when this intangible dwelling place
becomes tangible, when faith becomes sight.

I long for that true and complete freedom to come. C. S. Lewis
puts words to our longing:

> In speaking of this desire for our own far-off country, which we find
> in ourselves even now, I feel a certain shyness. I am almost commit-
> ting an indecency. I am trying to rip open the inconsolable secret in
> each one of you—the secret which hurts so much that you take your
> revenge on it by calling it names like Nostalgia and Romanticism
> and Adolescence. . . . Our commonest expedient is to call it beauty
> and behave as if that had settled the matter. . . . The books or the
> music in which we thought the beauty was located will betray us if
> we trust to them; it was not *in* them, it only came *through* them, and
> what came through them was longing. These things—the beauty,
> the memory of our own past—are good images of what we really

desire; but if they are mistaken for the thing itself, they turn into dumb idols, breaking the hearts of their worshippers. For they are not the thing itself; they are only the scent of a flower we have not found, the echo of a tune we have not heard, news from a country we have never yet visited.[4]

This is my true restless desire for home, and I announce my true home when I dwell in Christ and his grace. It's freeing that my security and comfort are not in things that change. I am meant for another place, and I am almost there. When I smell a smell or taste a taste that reminds me of a place I've called home, instead of feeling homesick for that place, I instead will turn my heart toward heaven. I will glory in the freedom that I have in Christ even now. And with Christ as my city, I can traipse all over this globe and never once not be at home.

Because I dwell in his grace.

Part Three

From Good to Grace

Responding

For the love of Christ compels us, because we judge thus: that if One died for all, then all died; and He died for all, that those who live should live no longer for themselves, but for Him who died for them and rose again.

2 Corinthians 5:14–15

7

Love Shows

WHERE THERE IS NEW LOVE, there is a makeover. At least that's what I've observed when a guy and a girl start dating and the guy has the fashion sense of a tree stump. As soon as the relationship moves into serious territory, the guy gets whisked away for a new haircut and an updated wardrobe to replace the athletic shorts and shirts that have held out since his freshman year of high school. He starts wearing hair gel and fashion-forward shoes. And, if he's really in love, perhaps even a belt.

I watched this happen with a guy I know. He started showing up *not* wearing his usual work uniform. He got a haircut and started tucking in his shirts. When my husband mentioned he was pursuing a woman, it all became crystal clear. I hadn't yet met her, but I had seen evidence of her existence in his wardrobe choices.

Love shows. When we love someone or something, it announces itself in our words, our time, our emotions, the way we structure our lives, and sometimes even in our hair gel.

God's love is no different. As we receive it, it absolutely will show itself. That's the thing about God's love: it's too big for us to contain. As we hold out our heart cups to receive, God's love naturally flows out onto others. We don't have to force it. If we receive it as he gives it, we *will* respond to it in some way, because God's love is compelling.

It's also dangerous. If we give ourselves to him, and open up our hearts to receive, he will compel us to love in ways we'd never choose or have the capability for on our own. Like sacrificially. Or biblically confronting a sister. Or caring for those who hate us.

Or forgiving.

There was a point in my life when I was wounded deeply by the words and actions of someone who had access to my heart. I wanted to tell everyone, and I wanted to hate the person who hurt me, and I wanted to count up all the ways the person had wounded me and cherish them in my heart. I felt so right in my anger, so sure of the offenses against me. The wounds mercilessly pounded away at my heart, and I shrunk inside myself.

Ironically, this wounding happened at the same time God was opening my eyes about the grace and love he'd offered me through Christ. I opened my hands and heart to receive, but each time I read Scripture or prayed, each time I thought about the person that hurt me, I recognized I had no right to receive it without also giving it; I had no right to hoard God's love. If I can receive it, wretched sinner that I am, it must, by its very nature, also be for others, even the one I wanted God to withhold it from. God's love was given to me, but it also induced me to go beyond simply receiving. Through process and time, always through his Word, his love compelled me to love the person who hurt me, which meant repenting of my anger and hatred and forgiving the offenses.

Love most definitely shows.

As we receive it, God's love works, and hard.

134

Eight Little Words

My goodness obsession, however, had *me* working hard for God's love for so long. It had me skipping ahead, trying to respond before receiving, trying to conjure up ways to prove my devotion to him. It had me laboring to make my own motivations for serving others. It had me in an emotional mess, attempting to be loved but never feeling assured that I actually was. It had me talking about personal action points but never about God's completed action on my behalf. I was the actor, the lover, and he was the object of my love. My goodness obsession never allowed him to be the lover, nor me to be the beloved.

Eight little words. That's all it took, just eight little words and, of course, the power of the Holy Spirit using them to pierce my heart.

We love him because he first loved us.[1]

That's the essence of the gospel boiled down into eight little words. Eight little words that changed the course of history, and changed the course of my history. This verse explains life, gives life, and is the goal of my life. It continues to inform and transform my heart as I wrestle with and grasp its ideas.

Eight little words about love—his love—boil further down to just one: *first.*

He *first* loved us.

I had this all so terribly wrong for so terribly long that it makes me want to weep. Just eight words—that's all I needed to get right— yet I colossally failed. I took those eight words, jumbled them up, and formed them into a nice, tidy formula lacking any of the words' original meaning: *Love God and then he will love you.*

This is a formula for disaster.

But I thought if I could make it work, if I were an excellent player in the game of good works, God would love me, really love me.

The formula—so tidy and pretty and clipboard official—didn't work.

Because I tried to love him first.

I tried to attain his love. It is a weird and useless endeavor trying to attain something you already have. By definition, love is a gift. It can never be forced or demanded or earned. We cannot attain love because God *is* love and we cannot attain God. His love is gifted to us. Our job is to receive it, devour it, enjoy it, and delight in it. When we receive it, we put down our checklist of good works and are soothed in our souls, to the very core of who we are. And then we exclaim "Aha!" in complete understanding, pick up the good works God has made us for, and carry on with a completely different motivation for those good works.

We are wanted.

We belong.

We are family members.

Fear no longer motivates us, because fear has been driven out by the overwhelming gift of God's love. We become motivated by love, that we might love him in response for the lavish love he has bestowed upon us. Certainly, we know our unworthiness of such a love, but we understand our unworthiness without any sense of fear. We know it, and it makes us glad because, like a diamond against a muted background, our unworthiness makes his love explode with more clarity.

Our human love between one another shows in conversation. It shows in affection. It shows in time and money spent. It alters life trajectories, choices, motivations, and thoughts. Love is powerful, powerful enough that it can't be contained or hidden. It always shows itself.

But when we are the loved? What joy! We walk light, we take care with our appearance because we are thought beautiful, we notice what they notice and love what they love. Being chosen does something to us.

How much more, then, does the love affect us when the love comes from God? How much more does it show itself when we are included in the Beloved? What happens when we taste God's love and grace and watch in awe as God pours himself into our hearts? His love cannot be contained, and it spills into our thoughts, motivations, and hopes and out in our conversations, affections, choices, and relationships. We are like cups under a running faucet: we grasp for what we can contain but our cup runs over, spilling out onto others. It shows and overflows. His love leaves marks; it makes us over.

God's love doesn't just overflow, however. It floods, and floodwaters make demands of what stands in their path. Floodwaters overcome, pushing down blocked doors, making their way through basements and closets, and tearing things from the walls.

The floodwaters of God's love will show themselves in the demands he makes on our lives. God's love demands to be the loudest voice, the final say, the death knell to what has come before. Regrets can't stand against it. Fear can't stand against it. Sin becomes impotent in its presence, in his presence. We cannot contain love and we cannot reach its end, but we can respond to the Love-Giver. And when we receive it, we absolutely *will*.

Do you believe that? Do you believe that God will compel you to love? Or do you believe that you must work yourself up to love others, that it's an obligation to fulfill? We are uncomfortable sitting too long in a receiving posture, afraid *not* to focus on loving and serving and doing. We want to jump immediately to the response without first receiving the love that compels. In our discomfort and agitation, we try dictating to God how he should be honored when he's already shown us the way. *Oh, Martha, you are distracted and anxious over many things. Mary has chosen right; she has chosen to receive first.*

When we know his love is *first*, that he loved us before we could do anything to earn it, our lives become a response of love. Instinctively, we fulfill the greatest commandments—to love God and to love others. But this type of enduring, persevering love can only happen when we first receive God's love.

We love because he first loved us.

He *first* loved.

And then that love shows through us.

How God's Love Shows

God's love leads us, first and foremost, to love him in return.

During the time that God's love became so real to me, and I concentrated on receiving it rather than striving for it, I remember a shift happening in my heart in regard to worship. Whereas I had once thought of worship as twenty minutes of singing on Sunday morning or as something I did to make God respond to me, I suddenly saw it for what it really is: a response unlimited by song choice or even by song itself. Worship is a life response to what God has already done, what he is currently doing, and what he has promised to do in the future. He is the actor; worship is my response to him and his action.

Receiving God's love always leads to worship. When we realize the extent to which he has gone to show us his love and to rescue us from our sin, we want to love him back. This isn't an obligatory or dutiful response but rather a joyful, willing response that flows from what we've received.

Worship develops into a craving for God. He is our safe place, the One whose wings we hide beneath. He is our companion, our security, our assurance. He is the truest peace we'll ever find. As we receive his care and loving provision for our soul's needs, we crave to be with him, and we treasure the Word where he beckons us to meet with him. Our desire is for him, and we devour Scripture looking for the ways he moves and speaks and loves.

Through this Word, he pours out his heart. As we receive it, we recognize a growing love for what he loves and we value what he values. Where are his eyes focused? For what and for whom does his heart race? As we receive him, our pulse races at the same things. We notice what our Lover notices, and we take joy in his joys.

Aside from his Word, his heart circles around one thing: people. Just as God's love worked through me to forgive the person who hurt me, it will show itself in how we relate to other people. We'll see a lessening concern for ourselves and a growing concern for others. The gospel waters seeds of self-denial and seeds of joyful service done in honor of Christ and for the benefit of others.

Scripture says it this way:

> For the love of Christ compels us, because we judge thus: that if One died for all, then all died; and He died for all, that those who live should live no longer for themselves, but for Him who died for them and rose again. (2 Cor. 5:14–15)

The love of Christ compels us to live for him. And how do we, in practical terms, live for him?

When asked about the greatest commandments—the most important things to God—Jesus replied,

> You shall love the LORD your God with all your heart, with all your soul, and with all your mind. This is the first and great commandment. And the second is like it: You shall love your neighbor as yourself. On these two commandments hang all the Law and the Prophets. (Matt. 22:37–40)

The second is like it. We love God by loving others. We cannot say we love God unless we love others as well.

The last part of the passage—that all the Law and Prophets hang on these two commandments—is interesting. Paul said something similar: "For all the law is fulfilled in one word, even in this: 'You shall love your neighbor as yourself'" (Gal. 5:14).

If all of the law is summed up in love, it seems that our greatest pursuit is to love. We respond to God's love by loving others and serving for their benefit.

We love him because he first loved us.

And we love others because he first loved us.

Joyful Service

God's love, then, is our motivation for service.

There are times when I find myself worn down from serving or dreading something I promised I'd do. Sometimes I'm frazzled and joyless in my service, and sometimes I don't love people very well or even like them very much. In those times, I can usually point to a salient moment when I chose to take on something that God himself was not asking me to take on. I signed up because I felt like I should or because I felt people expected it of me. I said yes because I wanted to impress people or because I knew I could do it and, well, why not? But then comes the weariness and the stress, and I'm reminded once again that my motivation was not God's love. In reality it was self-love.

God's love *must* be the motivation for our service or we turn instead to selfish ambition, obligation, pride, or any number of things that quickly grow burdensome and tiresome. We flame out, unable to persevere in the day in, day out faithfulness required to invest ourselves in the lives of others, because this type of service rarely feeds our self-centered motivations: few applaud, few are impressed, few even notice. Even obligatory service is selfishly motivated because we tend to silently applaud ourselves, having earned self-appointed brownie points for our good works. God needs us on his team, or so we tell ourselves.

Joyful service doesn't happen through impure motives, but it also doesn't happen through a certain strategy or step-by-step model. We must not be fooled or deceived into thinking God honoring service occurs according to a business paradigm or a perfectionist's checklist. If we subscribe to service as strategy it becomes a pressurized situation in which we must produce results at measurable intervals. The question, then, must be asked: Does the Spirit have room to move in our strategies? Does he even actually go near to our strategies?

Service is like life: it is not a formula.

Joyful service happens in the relationship of the server to her Savior, in which she comes to know the intricate details of her Savior and the grace and truth that flow from his heart. Out of this quiet, unseen fellowship, something supernatural happens. She is changed as she hears the voice of her Savior, and she is compelled by his love to engage in a ministry of reconciling others to her Savior.

Once the server has known the intimacy of the Savior, she cannot help but seek that intimacy for others. She receives ministry through relationship with him, and then she ministers through relationships. True service happens through messy, organic, give-and-take relationships, in which we give one another the truth and grace that we are receiving from our primary relationship with the Father.

And in interacting with people—living with them, bearing their burdens, listening to their doubts and heartaches, seeing the brokenness of the world—something supernatural happens. The server recognizes her inability to rescue or save or transform or make people whole, and she runs back to the One who does the actual ministry on behalf of his people. She receives and responds.

In regard to our primary relationship, Hudson Taylor writes:

> The intense activity of our times may lead us to be zealous in service but neglect personal intimacy with God. This neglect will not only lower the value of the service, but disable us for the highest service. . . . We must never forget that what we are is more important than what we do; that all fruit born when we're not abiding in Christ is fruit of the flesh, not of the Spirit.[2]

He goes on to describe the natural outflow of intimacy with God:

> Because she is one with the Good Shepherd, her heart goes instantly and by instinct to the feeding of the flock. She wants to walk in the footsteps of the one her soul loves. . . . Let her show her love to her Lord by feeding his sheep, by caring for his lambs. Then she need not fear she will miss his presence. When she shares with other under-shepherds in caring for his flock, she will find the chief Shepherd at her side and enjoy his approval. It will be service with Jesus as well as for Jesus.[3]

Joyful service is solely motivated by love—not our love toward God, as if we're showing him what we can do, but his love for us. It's based on a cyclical pattern of returning to Jesus, receiving from him, and then responding to him by loving others.

Free to Love

The only way we can love and serve others in this sustained way is to live as if our identity is being loved. This is actually our identity if we're in Christ, so that's very, very helpful, but how often do we think about that or truly believe it? I certainly don't wake up in the morning and feel refreshingly loved. I don't identify myself as "loved" to others because that would be weird, but I don't even often self-identify as loved. What I need, what we all need, is our identity proclaimed to us over and over again, so that we remember and so that we live from this truth about who we are.

The Bible is the mirror we look into each day, the proclamation we need that tells us we are loved because of what Jesus Christ did for us. We, then, must commune with God each day, to *remember* our identity, to read the proclamation, and to ask for the Holy Spirit's help to live out our identity as a member of the Beloved.

As we do this, the gospel has a freeing effect, because in the gospel the biggest questions and needs of life have been definitively answered. Are we loved? Yes, because of Christ. Do we belong? Yes, because of Christ. Are we approved? Yes, because of Christ. Are we righteous in God's sight? Yes, because of Christ. Do we have undying hope? Yes, because of Christ.

The lost world is still searching for clear answers to these questions. They're pouring time, energy, money, and their very lives out as they seek love, belonging, and redemption. But us? We already have the sweet assurance of Christ. We, then, are freed to love. We're free from a focus on being good and impressing others. We don't have to seek approval, so our energies can go toward love. We don't have to strive to be good enough, so we can strive to serve in the name of Christ and offer the answer to those who are seeking. It is actually by loving others that we announce our identity and home in the grace of Jesus Christ and invite others to join us there.

When we receive God's love and make a point to remember our "loved" identity in him each day, we find our perspectives on people changing. We look at others as parents look at their children: we see their possibilities and their giftedness, we want them to know they're loved, and we want the very best for them. We see our fellow believers as the new creations that they are and we're free to enjoy their uniqueness. We see those outside Christ with compassion and we long for them to also be free.

I've seen this in my own life. When I lived in my goodness obsession, I craved the love and approval of others. I practically *used* God and my good works to impress others and earn their admiration. I lived a spiritually isolated life, an individualistic life, because I both craved the validation of others and feared that I would not receive it. My energy and attention were constantly on these things.

But then God poured out his love, and I received it, and I started to see people differently. I read the book of Philemon and it struck me how the love of God brought a runaway slave and his former owner together as equals. Those people were changed by the love of God, and both the way they viewed each other and the way they interacted changed completely.

In my mind, I began to picture it like this: I imagined myself as a weak and beggarly woman crawling toward a pool of water. The water has healing powers for it is filled with an unending supply of the love of God. There at the edge of the water, I reached thirstily for what I believed would satisfy. And it did. It filled me, healed my wounds, washed me clean, and nurtured me. Though I was weak, dirty, and hopeless, God's love made me new.

But then I realized there were others there lapping up the water beside me. All around the pool, they were there.

Rich and poor.

Men and women.

Married and single.

Old and young.

The first world and the third.

Kings and paupers.

People with all manner of skin colors, languages, nationalities, abilities, and political ideologies.

In their need, they were devouring the life-giving love of God. Just like me.

Philemon shows that the love of God is the great equalizer. For who lives in more different worlds than a rich slave owner and his poor slave? At the cross of Jesus, the slave owner and the slave become brothers. The love of God *compels* them toward each other to offer the same mercy and grace that they themselves have received at the water's edge.

Without the love of God, we tend to regard other people with suspicion, as means to our own ends. We want to impress them.

We expect them to meet needs they can't meet. We want them to validate who we are and the choices we make.

But with the love of God giving us eyes to see and meeting every need we have, we no longer regard others by external categories or as means to our own ends. We regard them as co-sinners in need of grace or co-new-creations in Christ. We can enjoy others and champion them. We can offer belonging, acceptance, reconciliation, forgiveness, mercy, and grace. We can offer them God and his love that we ourselves have experienced.

Love in Weakness and Failure

Another freedom that our loved identity gives us is the freedom to reveal our weaknesses and let them be a catalyst for serving others. When we are loved by the ultimate Lover, we become less fearful of letting people really see us and know our pain, wounds, and sin.

When I lived according to my goodness gospel, I hid from people. I wouldn't let them see me cry or see that I didn't know what to do. I wasn't free to let God's power show in my weaknesses, because I couldn't admit my weaknesses even to myself and I definitely couldn't allow others to see that I didn't have it all together.

When God's love rushed in, I felt something relax inside of me. I dared to share my emotions and doubts and struggles with others, and even though not everyone responded how I wanted them to, I knew that God might use my freedom to invite others to be vulnerable, ask the hard questions, ask for help, and reveal their sin. It felt uncomfortable, and it still feels uncomfortable at times, but it also feels good to trust that God's power is made perfect in my weakness and to find, by my sharing, fellow grace-addicts who aren't just going through the motions. I've discovered that God gives us stories and thorns in our flesh to redeem and teach us but also to minister to others—if we share them. He best uses us to love and serve when we wrestle with real-life struggles out in the open. Because of God's love, we're free from having to hide our weaknesses and failures, and we're free to love.

This is risky, but it's purposeful. Our love for others must be purposeful, because Jesus was purposeful, and love motivated by God will always mirror the way Jesus loved.

I'm afraid our definition of how to love one another is skewed by our culture, or I suppose I should say that I'm afraid *my* definition of how to love is skewed by our culture. It seems to me that we want love to be easy and controlled and never to challenge our sensibilities. We don't want faithful people to call us into question, and if they do, we don't call it love. We don't want to have to give extravagantly, and we definitely don't want to get involved in the messiness of others' lives.

But Jesus didn't love like that. He pursued people constantly and said hard things. He interacted with people whom others considered lowlifes and expected nothing in return from anyone. He served sacrificially and impartially, concerned only for his Father's glory and our reconciliation to him.

It seems, then, that our love for others will be demonstrated in much the same way. We will pursue people and say hard things. We will interact with people whom others consider lowlifes and expect nothing in return from anyone. We will serve sacrificially and impartially, concerned only for our Father's glory and the reconciliation of others to him.

This is a tall order, but one that comes into view as we receive God's love and rely on the Spirit's direction and power. As we receive God's love, we recognize this is our *opportunity*, and it is not an obligation at all.

Who to Love

We've already established that God's love is a gift that is only fully received when we also give it away to others. They can't be separated, because we are receiving both an individual and a cor porate grace, and the individually received love from God leads to the corporately received love of God, and vice versa. Therefore, our seat at the table is among a multitude of others, the collective Beloved, and, though we are individuals beloved by God, we cannot fully know the love of God without the corporate Beloved.

The corporate Beloved, the Church, is the community in which we respond to God's love. We speak and are spoken to, we serve and are served, we teach and are taught, we help and are helped, we encourage and are encouraged, we challenge and are challenged. We receive and give the tangible ministry of Christ himself.

I love Ann Voskamp's description of how this mystery works. In *One Thousand Gifts*, she writes,

> *Eucharisteo* is giving thanks for grace. But in the breaking and giving of bread, in the washing of feet, Jesus makes it clear that *eucharisteo* is, yes, more: *it is giving grace away*. *Eucharisteo* is the hand that opens to receive grace, then, with thanks, breaks the bread; that moves out into the larger circle of life and washes the feet of the world with that grace. Without the breaking and giving, without the washing of feet, *eucharisteo* isn't complete. The communion service is only complete *in service*. Communion, by necessity, always leads us into community.[4]

This is not just signing up to work in the children's ministry because someone is needed. This isn't just praying for the sick because that's what we're supposed to do. This isn't *just* anything. The Church is our opportunity to give and receive the love of God. It's about relationships in which we sharpen and are sharpened. Our service is a vessel to pass the love of Christ among ourselves. This is our opportunity to tangibly give and receive love and grace to and from one another as a picture of the love and grace we've received from Christ. We are held accountable for our individual faith, but we experience his sanctification and sharpening through community, and we endure in our faith through the companionship of this community.

This picture of the Church eliminates any idea of it being a building or an institution that structures and employs programs. The Church is intended as a beautiful picture of Christ and his love. It's the multicolored wisdom of God, and each of us gets a hue. The specific community God's given us is our opportunity to respond to God's love according to the unique giftedness, personalities, and roles we've been given.

It's important to note that investing in community within the Beloved isn't something to add to a checklist of right Christian behaviors. Investing in community is a marker of whether we're receiving God's love and living in our loved identity, because the love of God *always* compels to what he loves, and he very much loves his Church.

Sent Ones

The love of God compels us toward and spills over into community, but it doesn't stop there. This love that moves from the individual to the Church then builds in strength to spill forth into the world.

Everything God does is for the redemption of sinners. He pursues, he seeks, and he offers new life in his Son to those who despise him, who have assaulted his name and reputation, and who have rejected his authority and his ways. His heart beats for them, and he longs for them to come to the table and enjoy true community with the Godhead. As we receive his love, we'll see this same desire developing in our hearts.

This is the where the collective Beloved responds to what's been received. They shall know us by our love—that's what Jesus said. They shall know us by how we give ourselves away to one another, how we gather around those of us who are hurting, how we are generous to share with one another, how we are reconciled to one another. In tandem with one another, each body part moving, we are a part of God's redemptive work in this world.

I like to think about the people in our church and how they're spread out all over our city, filling a variety of vocations, interacting with people from all walks of life. Some are doctors and nurses at the hospitals, some are teachers, some are stay-at-home moms, some are engineers, some are university students. Together, we are a swirl of activity and skills that take us into the lives of people Jesus is seeking. As we are purposeful to love one another and invite others into our relationships, we, through our love, invite them to join us at the table of redemption.

Again, this is not just a directive, a command, although we often whittle it down to obligation and duty. This is the directional flow of God's love, and it moves with explosive force. In other words, when we know the communion of God and the communion of saints, we cannot help but want to bring others who have not yet tasted and not yet seen into that communion.

If we're honest, we're so afraid of this. We want to stop up the flow of God's love and grace because we are fully aware that God's love flowing through us requires our stepping into messes and giving sacrificially and not having all the answers and being rejected or misunderstood or a million other things that make us uncomfortable. And what if grace isn't enough? What if God isn't enough in response to what we encounter in the world? What if we discover that he's not enough for *us*?

No, no, let's just sit in the glow of our community. Let's enjoy the comfort here. Let's not exert ourselves too much.

But how can God's love be held? Do we even know its fullness if we keep it to ourselves? Scripture seems to imply that it is only fully known and experienced when we talk about it, demonstrate it, and give it away to others. We awaken to the truth of God's love as we diffuse it to others.

To sit and grow fat on God's love and the love of others in community is to misunderstand the very identity he's given us as new creatures. We are the Sent Ones, witnesses of Christ. This is not just for some and this is not a suggestion. I dare say this is not even a command, as if we have a choice of whether or not to be who we are. We *are* the Sent Ones—this is who we are. This is not something to mull over, to decide whether we will be a witness or not. Just as we are Beloved, we are also Witnesses; it's just a matter of how we're living in that identity.

God's people have always been Sent Ones.

Abraham was the first Sent One: "I will bless you. . . and you shall be a blessing" (Gen. 12:2).

Jeremiah too: "For you shall go to all to whom I send you, and whatever I command you, you shall speak" (Jer. 1:7).

John was another Sent One: "There was a man sent from God, whose name was John. This man came for a witness, to bear witness of the Light, that all through him might believe. He was not that Light, but was sent to bear witness of that Light" (John 1:6–8).

The disciples were also Sent Ones: "You shall be witnesses to Me in Jerusalem, and in all Judea and Samaria, and to the end of the earth" (Acts 1:8).

Did you notice? They received, they paved a path, they told what they had heard and seen. Witnesses. But the work belonged to God, the Son, and the Holy Spirit. For us too God gladly takes the responsibility of salvation and sanctification. We are to simply receive God's love, take it with us to give to others, and witness to what we've received.

God's love is the fuel, the catalyst, the lifeblood for his Sent Ones. We go together, as the disciples did, and we go with the help of the Holy Spirit, as the disciples did. We are sent to where we are: our neighborhoods, our schools, our jobs, our families, our natural associations, and our relationships.

This is not a call to charge into the world to pierce darkness with conviction and truth. Again, that's the Holy Spirit's work. This is not a call to figure out how we're going to impact the world. We don't have to convince, and we don't have to plot and strategize. God's plan is already in motion and has been since Abraham set off toward a distant land. This is a call to love. This is a call to be faithful to live as a Sent One wherever God has placed us. This is a call to day in, day out faithfulness: to initiate a conversation, to make a meal, to listen to hard things, to extend grace, to work with diligence and excellence. A world-convincer gets tired, easily discouraged, and retreats quickly to lick his or her wounds among the already convinced. A witness knows the story must be told again and again, with different nuances for different perspectives. This isn't a big splash; this is a tiny pebble making a small ripple over and over again.

We don't have to charge into the world with truth-guns blazing, trying to protect our God. He doesn't need our protection, and his love doesn't compel us to rise up against the world anyway. The law compels us in that way, yes, but not grace. Not our God. His love compels us to see those outside the church with compassion, because that's how he saw us when we were outside. He stands over our Jerusalem and weeps with desire for its redemption. Do we separate ourselves from our Jerusalem or do we weep with him?

That we are Sent Ones is God's plan, and because it is his plan he blesses it. He will be victorious in it, and this is calming and freeing because, essentially, he is saying, *I am enough to carry out this plan.* The battle and the victory belong to him, but he offers us a role as Sent Ones.

Now thanks be to God who always leads us in triumph in Christ, and through us diffuses the fragrance of His knowledge in every place. For we are to God the fragrance of Christ among those who are being saved and among those who are perishing. To the one we are the aroma of death leading to death, and to the other the aroma of life leading to life. And who is sufficient for these things? For we are not, as so many, peddling the word of God; but as of sincerity, but as from God, we speak in the sight of God in Christ. (2 Cor. 2:14–17)

In this passage, Paul references a Roman triumphal procession following a victory in battle. The Roman general would parade his army and his captives through the city, celebrating having already conquered. Priests, holding censers filled with incense, would follow behind the conqueror in the procession. We, then, are the priests and Christ is the Conqueror leading us in procession.

The battle that has been won is not against flesh and blood but against principalities and powers. People are flesh and blood. Therefore, our battle is not against the people in this world. The gospel reminds us that we are all freed captives; we each know the experience of captivity. Through our fragrance—sharing the gospel in our love—Christ draws the perishing to life.

We cannot force any of this, because we can't force love.

But God will do it, deep in the unseen parts of our hearts. As his love seeps in and the floodwaters take down everything not of him, our hearts will well up and respond.

His love will compel us to love.

8

Giving Grace

WHEN THE ALARM CLOCK WENT OFF the morning after my wedding, I immediately bolted out of bed and dashed off to take a shower. We had a plane to catch, and I had to get the room straightened in preparation for checkout (because everyone does this, right?), so I was shocked when I returned from the shower to find Kyle still fast asleep, awaiting the second or third call of the alarm. I didn't know people actually used the snooze button, but evidently I had much to learn about my new husband.

After several mornings of this routine, Kyle turned to me during breakfast and said, "Do you always do that?"

"What?" I, of course, did everything right so I couldn't imagine why he sounded so mystified.

"Do you always pop out of bed like that? You are practically out of the bed the second the alarm goes off. It kind of scared me the first time. I thought something was seriously wrong when you jumped up like that."

We gaped at one another, his snooze button philosophy coming toe-to-toe with my up-and-at-'em philosophy. Who knew we'd experience our differences so early—literally and figuratively—in our marriage?

We quickly uncovered more. He squeezed every ounce of toothpaste from the tube by carefully flattening and rolling as he used it, while I just squeezed from wherever felt convenient in the moment—top, bottom, middle; whatever, man.

He constantly asked how long to heat his leftovers in the microwave, which, of course, drove me crazy because, really, how can you mess that up? Just pop it in and give it a go. Add a few seconds more if necessary. Or just blow on it if it's too hot. Whatever, man.

Sometimes, in those first few months of marriage, it felt as if both sets of our parents, along with their customs and habits, had moved in with us. All six of us were piled in our tiny seminary house, tripping over each other and playing tug-of-war over the minutiae of daily living. I could practically hear their voices in our arguments, "We do it this way!" "No, it is clearly done *this* way!"

Our families are different, and although we had dated for over three years before we got married, the differences we brought with us into marriage were still a bit shocking to us. It was tempting to label one another's preferences and customs as "right" or "wrong." It was also tempting to assume that once we made our rational, persuasive arguments for how we thought things should be done, the other one would see the brilliance of our position and immediately come to his/her senses.

Despite our best efforts, that pretty much never happened.

After several disagreements, surviving the first set of holidays, and making it through our first year of marriage, we eventually settled on traditions and ways of doing things that worked for the two of us as a fledgling family. But we learned lessons about one another and about our families that have served us well throughout our marriage, the main one being this: different isn't wrong. Different is just different. And different is even quite beautiful.

Unity or Uniformity?

When I stopped striving to earn grace and simply received it, I noticed an abrupt change in how I perceived and related to other people. What I had learned in our early months of marriage also informed my response to the unique ways God compelled those around me to love and serve others: different isn't wrong, different is just different, and different is even quite beautiful. God's grace allows for this, because God's grace brings profound unity among believers but also allows for freedom in how we respond to the grace we've been given. In Christ there is unity but not uniformity.

All of this sounds well and good, but in reality the application of this is where we—the goodness obsessed—have trouble. Too often, as we "run with endurance the race that is set before us," we look around at everyone else who is running alongside of us instead of "looking unto Jesus, the author and finisher of our faith."[1] We look to other Christians in order to determine how we're supposed to live or what our personal convictions should be. We look at their uniqueness and think it should be ours too. Or we look to other Christians and think they should be doing what we're doing. We turn our unity in the Beloved and like-minded purpose as Sent Ones into disunity and division, because we believe that the goal is uniformity.

When I walked according to the goodness gospel, for a good portion of my Christian life, I believed in uniformity. By its very nature, the goodness gospel requires uniformity and it leads us to judgment, huddling up according to our convictions, and isolating ourselves from others for fear of being judged. Because its greatest virtue is behavioral uniformity, the goodness gospel does not allow us to give grace to believers who are different from us.

This is why we too often find churches full of bitter, back-biting people. Believers can be cliquish according to their personal convictions and choices, unfriendly to outsiders, and critical of those who look or act differently than their chosen uniform cause. These characteristics are ungodly, a blatant sign of people who have never come to understand God's grace and love for them personally. They may know it intellectually but refuse it intimately and, therefore, cannot extend it to others.

Attitudes of ungraciousness betray an ignorance of God's grace, because his grace isn't selective nor is it selfish.

We are in good company, however, in our struggle to understand that the goal of God's grace is unity rather than uniformity: the apostle Peter also had a goodness gospel problem. After Jesus's resurrection, after he commissioned the disciples to go into the world with the gospel as Sent Ones, Jesus and Peter had an interesting and important interchange, one we can learn much from. As a sign of Christ's restoration of Peter, Jesus asked Peter three times, "Peter, do you love me?" Each time, Jesus equated Peter's love for him with loving and serving others. Having fully restored him, Jesus then prophesied somewhat ominously that Peter would die a difficult death in God's name. We see a clear progression of grace: Christ gave grace, Christ called Peter to give what he'd received, and then Christ gave Peter a specific way to respond to what he'd received.

Almost immediately, Peter turned around and looked at John: "But Lord, what about this man?" In other words, Peter wondered if John would die in a similar manner: "Aren't you calling him to the same thing?" Jesus's response to Peter is the same to us when we look around at others to compare or contrast our unique callings and convictions with theirs: "If I will that he remain till I come, what is that to you? You follow Me" (John 21:22).

We see from this exchange that receiving and giving grace means that our focus must remain on Jesus, that he will give each of us specific and unique ways to respond to that grace, and that he will often give other people *different* ways to respond to his grace.

His goal is our unity, not our uniformity.

A Terrible Dysfunction

What caused Peter to question his unique calling? He turned and looked at John.

Have you ever tried running next to someone while looking at them rather than looking straight ahead? Maybe it's just me, but I have to look where I'm going. If I don't, I trip, fall, or end up in someone else's lane.

We can't run our race well unless we look ahead to where we're going. Jesus is where we're going; he is our Finish Line. He wants us to look to him and run the race he's marked out for us. When we do that, we can't look around and compare.

We tend to assent with our minds that we are loved by God, that we are indwelt by the Spirit, and that we are approved by him, but we don't see how that applies to our relationships with others. We still compare and try to prove ourselves. We get our feelings hurt because people don't understand every nuance of our lives, our personalities, our circumstances, or our choices. We get frustrated and even offended that people aren't passionate about what we're passionate about. As a Church, we fight over trivial things. All because we're looking at our fellow runners and not at our Finish Line.

We call it something else. We call it a struggle: "I struggle with people-pleasing." We call it personality: "I can't help it. I'm a competitive person." We call it gender: "I'm a woman and women tend to compare themselves with other women." We call it personal conviction when it's really pride: "I am right and she is wrong." We call it low self-esteem: "I am nothing compared to her."

These are lies and have nothing to do with the gospel. The goodness gospel, yes. But the gospel of Jesus Christ? Absolutely not. However, as long as we continue to return to the goodness gospel, we will be enslaved to it, enslaved to a law that we can never perfect, and enslaving *others* to a law that *they* can never perfect.

If we live according to the goodness gospel, we will respond in comparison, competition, pride, self-condemnation, and jealousy. We will speak and teach the law, bringing others into bondage alongside us. We will cause division within the church. Serving others and ministering to others will become an absolute burden. We will be enslaved to the opinions and desires of others. And that, in fact, is the key of it all: if we live according to the goodness gospel, we aren't able to give away God's grace because we are looking to receive from others what we should be receiving from God—love, approval, acceptance, belonging, and guidance. We want to receive from people what they cannot possibly give. Other people are terrible gods.

The goodness gospel is a terrible dysfunction because it affects the individual but also affects the corporate Church. To illustrate, answer these questions:

> What is the right way: cloth or disposable diapers?
>
> What is the Christian way: private or public school?
>
> Who is the more spiritual mom: stay-at-home or working?
>
> What is right and what is wrong: missionary or businessperson?
>
> Who has favor in the eyes of God: single or married people?
>
> What is the right way to feed your child: organic or nonorganic?
>
> What is the right way to spend your money: give it to a good cause or go on a vacation?
>
> Who is the more spiritual: adoptive parents or those who have no children?

I'm curious as to your responses. However, I'm not looking for a circled list of right answers. This is not a biblical exam because this list does not cover any commands from Scripture. Of course, we could use Scripture to support our answers, but the Scriptures we'd choose are typically general principles that can be applied in different ways, not specific commands. This list does, however, cover things that we talk about in Christian circles. And we often make up rules about them.

If we set our lives according to man-made standards and parameters, we'll never be lonely. We can huddle together with the others who swear by cloth diapers and discuss the best brands. We can gather in our public school groups and turn our minds away from the unique needs of private school or home-school moms. We can go to the mission field and look pitifully at the Americans still sitting in the pews back home. Indeed, when we live by the goodness gospel, we can always find a like-minded soul to huddle with who will validate our choices. We can tell everyone our opinions as if they were law, because we have perpetual backup. We appear very together and very sure of ourselves.

But when we live according to the goodness gospel—these man-made standards that have no basis in the gospel—we huddle far from those who don't agree, who don't live as we do, or whom we cannot understand. We cause division because we force people into categories and identities based on their choices.

When we live according to Christ's gospel of grace, we may be lonely in the sense that we won't huddle in any one category. We aren't identified by our choices. We can't be put in a box. We identify ourselves not as this kind of mom or that kind of woman but as a child of God, as Beloved. We follow his lead, not the lead of the huddle we're in.

Living identified as a child of God is hard to do. It's really hard to walk in grace. It's really hard to extend it to others who are different than we are. It's hard because we have to reject the comparison game, and our flesh was born to compare. It's hard because we can't settle into nice, neat little categories, and we risk being misunderstood or judged. It's hard because sometimes God leads us differently than how he leads others, and we're standing out on an island feeling both vulnerable and, sometimes, like we're doing something wrong or completely unspiritual.

But in another sense, grace is not lonely at all. Grace attracts where the law repels and divides. More accurately, grace attracts those *who know their need for it*, and it repels those who think they've already got it all figured out. A person living in grace will never be without the companionship of the fellow poor-in-spirit. Many will be drawn and freed by the grace she speaks.

So how did you answer the questions above? Each question should make you rise up in frustration, not rise up to defend your position, because these aren't the right questions we should be asking anyway. They aren't the questions we should be talking about with other women. They aren't the most important things. Instead, we should be thinking about the humility that comes out of understanding the gospel; we should be talking about faith, hope, and love far more than diapers, education, and marriage; and we should be encouraging one another to go to God to ask, "Lord, what is it you have for me as an individual or for us as a family?" and then rejoicing in God's clear answers.

Grace brings unity, but it doesn't bring uniformity.

A push toward uniformity just produces evidence of the flesh as described in Galatians 5:19–21: idolatry, hatred, contentions, jealousies, selfish ambitions, dissensions, and envy. Walking in the Spirit and by faith will take you to the heart of God, but it will not lead you to pride, exclusivity, elitism, or the unbiblical judgment of others. If it leads you to become a Pharisee, it's self-sufficiency, not the Spirit.

When we know grace, however, we respond with grace. The law causes us to look to other people for selfish gain but the gospel

allows us to give to others without any need for return. Grace
received leads us to love, to be compassionate, and to offer grace
to others. We will have a longing for others to experience the joy
and love and freedom we've experienced.

How exactly, then, do we give grace?

Grace Gets Specific

To give away grace, we must first understand the general call to
unity and how that leads to specific and individual responses.

At the core level, of course, the gospel leaves no room for differences. Scripture makes it clear: *All* have sinned. *All* fall short of
the glory of God. *No one* can be justified by the law in the sight
of God. Christ lived a perfect life, then died, taking the just wrath
of God and imputing his righteousness for *all* those who believe.
All are called to repentance and to faith, and *all* who come are
given new life in Christ's resurrection.

> For you are all sons of God through faith in Christ Jesus. For as many
> of you as were baptized into Christ have put on Christ. There is
> neither Jew nor Greek, there is neither slave nor free, there is neither
> male nor female; for you are all one in Christ Jesus. (Gal. 3:26–28)

Although those who believe in Christ are one at the gospel level,
we still retain our "Jewishness" or "Greekness" and our "maleness"
or "femaleness." We retain the differences that give us access and
opportunity to give to others what we ourselves have received in
Christ. And our responses of worship will be as individual and as
unique as we are created individual and unique.

It's clear we are to give away what we've received. We see it and
hear it from Jesus himself. He washed the disciples' feet and then
commanded them to follow his example. His command wasn't to
actually go around washing feet, but his command was for them

to serve in the same manner and with the same heart with which they had been served. The command was general, but the disciples obeyed it according to their unique gifts, personalities, and circumstances. Some were teachers, so they taught. Some were writers, so they wrote. Some were analytical, some were emotional and passionate. But all gave away what Jesus had first given them.

In Paul's writings, we see a corporateness, a unifying element, to our faith in Christ. He gave the general call of unity under the gospel to the church at Ephesus: "I . . . beseech you to walk worthy of the calling with which you were called . . . endeavoring to keep the unity of the Spirit in the bond of peace. There is one body and one Spirit, just as you were called in one hope of your calling; one Lord, one faith, one baptism; one God and Father of all" (Eph. 4:1–6). But then he followed those words with these: "But to each one of us grace was given according to the measure of Christ's gift" (v. 7). As children of God, we are called to receive and give God's grace. But the manner in which we give it is unique, individual, and specific according to the measure God has chosen to give us.

In Paul's description of the Church as a body in 1 Corinthians 12, we see how both unity and uniqueness work together. With Christ as our Head, we move in unity to serve the greater good and portray Christ to our world, but each of us is a unique member placed by the Holy Spirit in the one Body.

This is why we cannot live the Christian life apart from the Holy Spirit. Where the law, before Christ, tried to keep us within parameters according to rules and regulations—which, by the way, only held a mirror to our sinful hearts and taught us that we needed something more to help us—we now live by the Holy Spirit. He has circumcised our hearts, written the law there, and now guides, convicts, and counsels us. God himself is our parameter. The Holy Spirit indwelling us is a gift of grace, and he promises to convict of sin, provide a way out of temptation, and lead us to the good works God has planned for us according to the gifts he's given us.

The spiritual gifts he imparts are gifts of grace, and the fact that they are individual and specific to each person is also a gift of grace. There is an additional theological layer to add, found in Acts 17:

> God, who made the world and everything in it . . . gives to all life, breath, and all things. And He has made from one blood every nation of men to dwell on all the face of the earth, and has determined their preappointed times and the boundaries of their dwellings, so that they should seek the Lord. (vv. 24–27)

These verses give us the theology we teach to even the youngest of our children: God made us and appointed our days. Because he made us, he made our personalities. Because he appointed our cultural backgrounds and the places we live, he has chosen for us the best circumstances in which we can know and receive new life in Christ and, therefore, in which we can give what we have received. So we know this:

The gospel is for all, is needed by all, and is encountered by all the same.

We are all called to give to others what we have been given in Christ.

We are unified by our faith in Christ, and we move as one Body.

Within our unity, because God has made us unique, has appointed us to unique circumstances, and has given us unique spiritual gifts through his Spirit, his grace allows for differences in the ways we serve and love God.

In other words, we run the race of faith with other runners, but we each run the unique race that God has marked out for us.

To give the grace we have received means that we live well in our differences, we think grace toward one another, we speak grace toward one another, and we give grace to one another according to our individual gifts.

Thinking Grace

Thinking on the grace that we've been given in Christ helps us to think about others through the lens of God's grace. We must give ourselves to thinking on grace, meditating on grace, and considering how it applies to our everyday lives, so that when we relate to others we have much to draw from. We have eyes of grace for others.

Over coffee and blossoming friendship, Susan and I shared our stories, our fears, and the victories we've experienced in Christ. Just before I had to leave, I remembered a specific decision was weighing on her and asked about it: "Have you made a decision about your kids and school?"

She nodded, indicating they had decided to make a change. I could tell she felt a little uncomfortable, nervous even, and I knew why. Our kids went to school together. We were alike, and her decision was about to make us different. Would I receive that as an indictment of my own choice?

Susan is a woman of deep faith, and I knew she had sought the Lord's direction through prayer for many months. "That's wonderful," I said, "I am so happy for you that God has made it clear!"

There was a time, however, when I struggled when others in our church made choices different from my own. I worried I was not spiritual enough or that others were judging me or that perhaps I was actually missing what God was saying to me. I wrestled in prayer, rehashing over and over with God what he had already laid out clearly.

I've found that my discomfort with differences is not unusual among women in the church. Our greatest struggles and misunderstandings are typically concerned with open-ended issues such as education choices, working/nonworking choices, financial choices, and parenting practices. As a result, we self-divide, huddling into groups that share our convictions and can best relate to us. We create further division when we evaluate and judge others based upon these convictions.

But it all comes back to grace. In my thoughts toward Susan, it came back to grace. Would I accept that God might have me do something different than my godly friend? Could I champion her decision while also feeling free in my own? The only way I could do that would be to receive God's grace, set my eyes on my Finish Line, and be obedient to how he, by his Holy Spirit, asked me specifically to respond.

I return again and again to Romans 14 because it helps me know grace, think about grace, and think grace toward others regarding these issues:

> For one believes he may eat all things, but he who is weak eats only vegetables. Let not him who eats despise him who does not eat, and let not him who does not eat judge him who eats; for God has received him. Who are you to judge another's servant? To his own master he stands or falls. . . . For none of us lives to himself, and no one dies to himself. For if we live, we live to the Lord; and if we die, we die to the Lord. Therefore, whether we live or die, we are the Lord's. For to this end Christ died and rose and lived again, that He might be Lord of both the dead and the living. But why do you judge your brother? Or why do you show contempt for your brother? For we shall all stand before the judgment seat of Christ. . . . So then each of us shall give account of himself to God. (Rom. 14:2–4, 7–10, 12)

Paul tells us that a grace-filled response will allow for differences on open-ended issues. We don't all have to do everything the same way. Each of us lives by faith as unto the Lord, and we will account only to God for how we lived in response to him. Because of this, we aren't to judge others who think differently on these issues. Just as we trust God to lead us, we must trust God to lead others.

That said, grace gives us more to think about:

Therefore let us not judge one another anymore, but rather resolve this, not to put a stumbling block or a cause to fall in our brother's way. I know and am convinced by the Lord Jesus that there is nothing unclean of itself; but to him who considers anything to be unclean, to him it is unclean. Yet if your brother is grieved because of your food, you are no longer walking in love. Do not destroy with your food the one for whom Christ died. . . . Do not destroy the work of God for the sake of food. (vv. 13–15, 20)

Grace and the freedom it offers us should always benefit others; it is not for our benefit and our freedom alone. Paul writes, "For you, brethren, have been called to liberty; only do not use liberty as an opportunity for the flesh, but through love serve one another" (Gal. 5:13). In other words, we must live in responsible freedom, not taking advantage of God's grace by living for ourselves, not mocking grace through blatant sin and taking opportunities for our flesh, and not taking lightly the impact we have on others around us. It also means that we don't hold up our personal convictions as the only right way.

Some may be offended or distraught by the idea that their freedom is limited by others around them. But Paul, even though he had freedom through the grace of Christ, said, "For though I am free from all men, I have made myself a servant to all, that I might win the more" (1 Cor. 9:19) and encouraged every believer to concentrate on edifying others, Christian or not. In 1 Corinthians 10:23–24 he said, "All things are lawful for me, but not all things are helpful; all things are lawful for me, but not all things edify. Let no one seek his own, but each one the other's well-being."

In our Christ-given freedom, we have the opportunity and responsibility to use it to impact the kingdom of God. When we are set free from slavery to our sin, invited to the banqueting table as a child of God, and have experienced the love of God, we cannot help responding in kind to him and to share that powerful love and grace with others. We also are eager and willing to set aside some of our Christ-given freedoms in order that we might reach others all the more. This attitude is a clear sign of a grace-minded child of God, knowing that we retain no ownership over ourselves and that the freedom we've received through God's grace is not *just* for us.

If our convictions cause grief or cause another to stumble, we aren't walking in love or grace. In other words, our freedom isn't the highest priority in the kingdom of God and we aren't to flaunt it. We aren't to put our convictions above love.

So we must think about how grace applies to others, not just how it applies to ourselves. When we think about grace for other people, we cross false boundaries that keep us apart, we see more quickly what unifies us rather than what makes us different, we focus on what is truly at the heart of the kingdom of God, and—this is where it gets really exciting—we're able to speak grace into the lives of others who are weary, dry, and desperate for it.

Speaking Grace

When we share with others and enter into their lives, God's grace and Christ's role as Leader and Conqueror allow us the freedom to not always have a packaged answer or even an answer at all. Grace grants us the ability to not force ourselves onto others or set law-imitating standards of behavior for people, because we believe God is powerful, God will act, and God will convict. Our Conqueror goes before us, and his Spirit can change hearts.

I haven't always gotten this right. I've been judgmental toward the world and afraid of the world, precisely because I haven't understood the power and sufficiency of grace. But I've seen that when I receive God's grace and trust his hand, it frees me to enter the doubts and questions of others with confidence and peace. I'm just following the lead of my Conqueror and extolling the beauty and power of his grace. I don't have to convince or convict.

One girl with whom I've spent time discussing matters of faith, God's love, and obedience recently sent me this note:

> So many people I've encountered have told me how to live and what I should be doing. Most people take the opportunity to tell other people what and how to do something, usually the way they do things. You haven't done that to me. I will never forget you saying, "I'm not going to tell you to [modify a behavior], because I trust that the Holy Spirit will tell you that." You really trust the Lord that he is alive and active. You trust that his Word is true and that he will work in his time.

We have countless opportunities to encourage others, to share the gospel with others, to answer questions, and to counsel others. Each of those moments is an opportunity to speak grace. But we have to be careful that we are speaking grace, because if we are living by the goodness gospel we'll give them the goodness gospel.

We can give them law or we can give them grace. When others seek our counsel, we can focus on external rules or we can focus on the heart. When we offer them words of wisdom, we can give them advice and a checklist or we can exhort them to seek out the Lord's direction and obey his voice. When we have opportunity to minister in Christ's name, we can put our confidence for ministry in ourselves or we can put our confidence in the power of the Holy Spirit and the power of the gospel.

The ministry of the law is easier. It's much simpler and requires much less process and faith to put rules and parameters into place that have no power to touch the heart. When those seeking our wisdom take it and apply it with good results, we feel pretty good about what we're doing and the impact we're making, and everything is very cut-and-dried.

The ministry of the law provides no value against temptation, however, other than showing us that we cannot save ourselves. The ministry of the law is the ministry of death and condemnation. We simply can't bring people to a list of Christian morals, rules, and regulations and leave them there.

We must give them grace, as found in Christ's gospel. We must know it, be able to speak it to ourselves, and also be able to speak it to others.

Our ministry must be the ministry of the Spirit, the ministry of life, freedom, and righteousness. And isn't righteousness, especially, the desired result of any wisdom, counsel, or advice we give? We are so afraid *not* to give rules and regulations because we're afraid of people cheapening grace. The ministry of the Spirit, however, *leads* to righteousness and joyful obedience.

So why is the ministry of the Spirit more difficult? Because we have to place our confidence in our unseen God, and we—both the counselors and the counselees—have to trust God to speak and obey him when he does. We can't rely on easily set-up (and easily dismantled) man-made parameters to keep our hearts in line. We have to be willing to walk in the process of transformation with those we counsel. We have to rely on God to do what only he can do in a heart. We have to know and hold firmly to the truth that we are transformed only by the Spirit of God.

When we respond to the grace we've received by speaking it, we'll have plenty of opportunities with believers and nonbelievers alike. The aroma of grace is like a magnet: it attracts others because we effuse a full assurance that God and his grace are sufficient. Grace is strong. We can live authentically before others, believers and nonbelievers, because our trust is in God and not in ourselves. We can struggle, we can doubt, we can cry, and we can fail—and in all these things we don't have to hide because grace is big and Christ is Conqueror.

If grace is a magnet that attracts, there are two main ways to repel the world: require others to live according to law or live according to the law ourselves. The law does to others what it does to us—it weighs down with condemnation, guilt, and pride. There is nothing compelling about a set of rules or a checklist of behaviors. If we hold on to the law as a backup in case grace fails, we're basically saying to the world that Christ isn't enough.

We only diffuse Christ when we diffuse grace.

And Christ is compelling.

Giving Grace

Grace turns our eyes to the Grace-Giver and it compels us to *run* toward him with joy and passion and abandon. As we live in grace, this is where we experience the abundant life, and this is where things get really exciting! Because when our lives are lived for him in response to the grace he's given us, we don't have to worry about fitting into a "goodness" mold. When our eyes are locked to his, we realize we're free from dutiful obligation and free to be who we are to the glory of God. We have the opportunity to squeeze every ounce out of our personalities, our circumstances, our spiritual gifts, our obedience, and our passions in order to honor him. We realize that perhaps what we love and what we're gifted for are actually God-given and can be used joyfully for him. And we can rest in how God chooses to use us to edify the Body of Christ and accomplish his purposes. We don't have to be timid, we don't feel like we have to be someone else, and we don't have to worry that we're not doing enough or enough of the right things. This is responding to grace. This is living in grace.

In Titus, Paul says that those who live in accordance with their new nature in Christ, shown by their obedience to God and their good works, "adorn" the gospel (2:10). When we live by the grace of Christ, when we run with reverence and joy the race he has marked out for us, we show the beauty of the gospel. We are like artists, all creating in different mediums to display the loveliness and wonder of the grace Christ offers all those who believe. And just as artists create unique to their talents and perspectives, our adornment of the gospel will be unique to each of us.

Our unity comes in Christ and so our one goal as unique artists is to draw eyes to Christ. We miss grace entirely if we think we are the end of grace, as if the beauty is in our own uniqueness or our own freedom. We don't serve to draw eyes to us or to adorn ourselves. Grace demonstrated to others draws their eyes to admire the beauty and truth of Christ. Our goal, remember, is to follow our Conqueror, diffusing the fragrance of his grace.

Recently, in our church small group, we were discussing how we could, as a group, live missionally in our city. How could we best do that? Where should we focus our time and attention? Where were others already connecting and earning credibility in our city and how could we join them there? It was somewhat of a frustrating discussion because we couldn't come to any certain conclusion. Some were concerned for the refugees in our city, some were connecting in their neighborhoods and schools, and others brought up their coworkers and the university campus. Some thought we should meet tangible needs, some thought straight-up evangelism was best, and some kept coming back to the importance of hospitality in our homes. Finally, we saw what was happening: everyone was answering according to their life circumstances, their personalities, their spiritual gifts, and their passions. We would never come to uniformity because we weren't meant to. We will all adorn the gospel in different ways, and different is not wrong. Grace allows for those differences and even invites those differences so that we will all reach into different corners of the world with our one message.

As you look to the Lord and let his grace put your legs in motion, how is he nudging you to adorn the gospel? This is how you will give grace.

What spiritual gifts has he given you?

> Having then gifts differing according to the grace that is given to us, let us use them: if prophecy, let us prophesy in proportion to our faith; or ministry, let us use it in our ministering; he who teaches, in teaching; he who exhorts, in exhortation; he who gives, with liberality; he who leads, with diligence; he who shows mercy, with cheerfulness. (Rom. 12:6–8)

In other words, stir up your gifts and be passionate about using them to the glory of God!

Where do you find yourself in life? Most certainly, the Lord intends you to adorn the gospel in whatever roles you fill, whatever life stage you currently find yourself, and whatever circumstance you're facing. But how, specifically? God owns your time, your money, your work, your children, and your very life. How does he want you to steward what he has given you to adorn the gospel?

What is your personality? Are you a go-getter or a behind-the-scenes kind of person? Extrovert or introvert? What do you love and what comes easily to you? What passions are stirring deep in your heart, wanting to get out? All of these things about you can be used to adorn the gospel.

The point is that our lives belong to God. About this we can be certain: he will lead us perfectly as we focus our eyes on the Finish Line. *We don't have to figure things out.* We've been given the Holy Spirit.

We must be careful, because the goodness gospel can infect everything, even the gifts God has given us. If we aren't meditating on the gospel each day, we tend to live by works, performing for ourselves (and others) and trying to author our own righteousness and good works. We do a poor job of both apart from the Spirit. So why do we still try? Why can we not hold fast to the freedom we've been given in Christ? How can we live life by faith and through grace?

When we put our religious checklist down and back away slowly, when we turn our hearts back toward the gospel, what we're left with is the authorship of God. How is he leading me? How is he leading you? What gifts has he given us and how does he want us to use them?

Ephesians 2:10 describes God's authorship with a beautiful word picture: "For we are His workmanship, created in Christ Jesus for good works." The original language says, "We are God's poem." God is not just the author of my salvation and good works, he is a poet who, if I stop striving and attempting to work in my own strength, creates a work of art in my heart and through my hands.

Not coincidentally, this imagery follows Paul's adamant declaration that our salvation and anything that follows that salvation have occurred entirely because of God's grace. Just as God is the author of my newness in Christ, he is the author of everything that has come and will follow. By my efforts, I author a powerless tale of fruitlessness. But when I allow God to author my life and good works, he writes a poem with my life—an unexpected, beautiful, and specific-to-me poem.

He is the Author of grace, and we adorn that gospel with our good works. We can trust him to lead us to those good works.

Joy!

If God authors our adornment of the gospel, we see immediately that this kills all comparison, competition, and judgment between all who are running alongside us. Instead, we are able to celebrate others and how God is authoring their adornment of the gospel. We encourage them to listen for the Lord's leading and to step out in faith rather than encouraging them to respond to God just like we do. We want them to run the race full steam ahead, powered by his grace. We receive grace, and we give it, and that's what it looks like. There is so much joy when we live in grace!

A friend told me about a new little resale boutique in the neighborhood, and since the weather kept announcing it was time to pull out the fall clothes, I popped in to see what sweaters and boots I could find to fill out my wardrobe. Though the store was neatly and attractively arranged with racks of seasonally assorted clothes and shelves showing off shoes like the house-sized closets I've seen on television, I was the only customer.

The woman behind the counter greeted me, and I knew instinctively that she was the owner of the boutique. Locally owned boutiques make me nervous for this very reason: the owner is usually standing behind the counter, there are typically only a handful of customers coming in and out, and I feel an instant kinship with the owner and a strange compulsion to rally behind them. I find myself internally cheering them on because I want them to succeed at something they clearly feel passionate about, which means I usually buy something.

I browsed the racks, tried a few things on, and noticed everything. Because I also do this weird observation thing in small boutiques: I think about how the owners choose their displays and how they lay out their stores. I imagine the owner making decisions about everything from fitting rooms to merchandise to marketing. I almost enjoy this part of shopping—the noticing part—more than I do the actual shopping for clothes. I suppose I love seeing other people's passions being pursued. It's an artist appreciating another's art, a joy derived from another's joy, my passion feeding off and growing from another's passion.

I, of course, bought something from the lady behind the counter—a cute tangerine jacket. Tangerine, the color of joy and passion. And I left thinking about the lady. What was she doing in her empty store after I had gone? I imagined her tidying the racks, restocking the clothes I had tried on and not wanted, preparing more shoes for the glamorous shelves. I wondered what she thought about as she stood in her empty store, waiting for customers. Was she discouraged? What made her feel like things would work out after all? Probably she has moments of sheer panic and emotional flailing, but then she goes right back to prepping clothes and thinking of marketing strategies. *Take that, discouragement!*

She returns to what she loves to do, because she loves it and she can't not do it. *She goes back to the joy of pursuing her passion.* Because it's not likely that anyone is coming in and exclaiming, "I'm so glad you're here! I've been waiting for you to sell second-hand clothes in this space all my life!" It's not likely that anyone is affirming her passion or holding her hand through those moments of sheer panic. I'm also pretty certain people aren't stampeding to her door to say thank you or to make spirit tunnels for her to run through at the end of the day after she's vacuumed the floor and locked up for the thousandth time.

This is what I'm getting at: joy isn't in the response of others based on what we do. Joy is in doing what God created us to do and has given us to do. Joy is in pursuing with faith and abandon the passions God has laid in our hearts, and doing them in his honor. We serve for the smile on his face.

And joy begets joy. When we serve God with joy, we in a roundabout way encourage others to serve God with joy. Artists appreciate another's art, joy is derived from another's joy, and passion feeds off and grows from another's passion.

So whatever you're doing—homeschooling, event planning, cake baking, medical research, substitute teaching, diaper changing, coaching, putting words out into the world, or, yes, running a small boutique—do it with joy as unto the Lord. Don't look for appreciation from others or a spirit tunnel at the end of the day as an indicator of whether or not you're on the right track. Look to God, who created you to be a creator that flings tangerine passion and joy into the world. *He is smiling as you do what you do for him.*

There is no mold, no one right way of showing Jesus, for where the Spirit is, there is freedom.

He has made us each different, combining us all to make a collage, a collage that when you step back and look you suddenly see: it's Jesus!

Different mediums.

Different brushes.

Different strokes for reaching different folks.

You there, with your unique talents, passions, and gifts.

Go in freedom.

Tell them about Jesus with your life.

Do it with grace and tangerine joy.

9

We Hope

A S CHILDREN, MY SISTER AND I would recreate our favorite game show, *The Price Is Right*, and pretend to be detectives searching for the bad guys just like our favorite cop show heroines, Cagney and Lacey. Our driveway made the perfect roller-skating rink on which to choreograph routines to the *Footloose* soundtrack or to Whitney Houston singing that she wanted to dance with somebody. At our grandparents' house we made tiered mud pies resembling wedding cakes, and at home we rushed around seating invisible people at our pretend restaurant, passing out homemade menus, taking orders, and laying out plates of plastic food. Every year, we stayed up late to watch the Miss America pageant and after the climactic moment when the winner was crowned, wrapped blankets around our waists as gowns, draped long-sleeved shirts on our heads as flowing hair, and pranced gracefully around the living room pretending to be beauty queens.

Our favorite game was "MASH," a silly game all of us girls played where we made predictions about any number of things: whom we would marry, how many kids we would have, and whether we'd live in a mansion or a shack. When the MASH game predicted I'd marry the dorkiest guy in school and live with him and our hundred children in a shack, I'd just laugh and start over. The future I envisioned held only good things.

Hopes that are no hopes at all eventually show themselves. Dreams of a future secured by winning the showcase showdown, having a glamorous job, being skinny and beautiful, becoming famous, or being swept away by a handsome man to the MASH-predicted mansion are bait-and-switch kind of dreams. Like trying to grasp the wind, as one wise man once said.

But of course as we grew up our hopes became tempered by time, experience, maturity, and perhaps a little cynicism. We choose the realistic hopes now, the predictable things: marriage, children, friendship, youth, adventure (or at least a vacation every once in a while), fulfilling work, health, retirement.

But are these true hopes? They are incredibly good gifts, yes, but are they worthy of our hope? If these are our hopes, the end of our desires, what happens when spouses disappoint, children become prodigals, friendships fall apart, beauty doesn't age well, jobs are mundane or taken away entirely, or health fails? If these are our hopes, they will eventually shatter.

I know, because my hopes have been shattered into a million little pieces.

And it was one of the best things that ever happened to me.

Shattered

I didn't know a two-year-old was capable of sentences and dressing himself. I didn't know two-year-olds could interact so profoundly with the world and the people in it. I felt stupid for not knowing. When the diagnosis came, I felt as if everyone else had known but hadn't wanted to tell me for fear of hurting my feelings. I missed the small signs: his lack of pointing, he didn't bring things to me he was interested in as an act of connection, and he didn't wave good-bye to friends and family.

I only saw the positives. Though he couldn't tell the woman at the library his name or age, or even sit still long enough for her to look him in the eye and ask the questions, when I pushed him in the swing, he said the alphabet and recited his favorite book, *Chicka Chicka Boom Boom*, at lightning speed. He counted to twenty before age two and pointed out the numbers on the speed limit signs along the road. He knew his colors and consistently repeated lines from his *VeggieTales* videos.

But when the diagnosis came—autism—I suddenly saw it everywhere.

I saw it all too clearly when we went to parents' night at his new preschool. We'd been invited into the classroom to see what the kids had been learning and to become familiar with school routines. As soon as we entered the school and saw the artwork hung above the coat hooks, trepidation swept over me. We could pick out our son's artwork easily. The others had carefully painted flowers or drawn stick-figure family members, but he had simply taken a brush, jerked it down the page, and been pleased enough with his work to leave it at that. When we entered his classroom, it was the same. Nothing of his things said, "I have a personality" or even "I am clued in to what is happening here." Instead, we saw a list posted on the cabinet to remind the teachers which hand each child used to cut with scissors. His was blank.

Kyle and I sat in our car in the parking lot for an hour crying and screaming in pain. We cried because we grieved all that we were losing. The idea of who our son was and the dreams we had for him were shattered, just as the dream of what our family could be had died. We grieved over the uncertainty of our son's future. The spectrum that autism diagnoses cover is so vast, and we didn't know where he would land on that spectrum. Would he be with us for the rest of his life, not able to express himself or dress himself? Or would his affinity for numbers and technology make him the next Bill Gates? Would he marry and have children, or would he be a social outcast? As much as we wanted answers, all we had was our overwhelming grief.

My first response was to fight. I fought against the autism itself. I fought to return to some sort of normalcy. I fought to bring our son "out of it." But mostly I fought against God, holding tightly to a false hope that if I worked hard enough, the scales would tip in my favor and the autism would go away.

I wrestled with the life God had given me. I was disappointed because this wasn't what I had envisioned for my family, this wasn't a part of the script I'd written for myself. I was disappointed by my false hopes and by how quickly they had let me down.

The dream had died and I needed a new dream, one built upon true and enduring hope. I recognized that my shattered hopes had been built upon my own control, my own ability to create the life I wanted, and my own comfort. They had been built upon my foundational belief that God was obligated to give me what I felt I deserved. They had, above all, been built upon the goodness gospel.

Where the Goodness Gospel Can't Go

Let me tell you, the goodness gospel only walks with you so far. The goodness gospel is a friend as long as life is neat and tidy, as long as we have it all lined up how we want it. The goodness gospel tells us that we're in control of our circumstances, that we can earn the life we desire, that our circumstances give evidence to the level of our obedience and faithfulness, and that if we're good enough we won't suffer or even be disappointed in the slightest.

It tells us we don't deserve pain because we've tried to be good, so it won't walk with us through suffering or difficulty or disappointment. It's not strong enough to hold up under the questions and the burdens and the grief and the pressure. The goodness gospel lays the weight on us to create our own hope, and when we cling to it in our suffering we direct our anger at God, become bitter people, and fall apart completely. We don't have hope.

In Jesus's day, the religious company line was that suffering and sickness were the result of sin. If a man was wealthy, it was a sign of God's blessing. If a woman was barren, it was a sign of God withholding blessing because of her sin.

Jesus constantly tore down these arguments, my favorite being this exchange with his disciples:

> Now as Jesus passed by, He saw a man who was blind from birth. And His disciples asked Him, saying, "Rabbi, who sinned, this man or his parents, that he was born blind?" Jesus answered, "Neither this man nor his parents sinned, but that the works of God should be revealed in him." (John 9:1–3)

Even the disciples believed this line of thought: *If we're good enough, God will bless us. We won't have to suffer.* Isn't that so like us? It reveals our greatest goal is control and our most beloved idols are comfort and happiness.

But Jesus taught something dramatically different. He taught that the world is broken and that no one will escape the fruits of this brokenness, not even he himself, the Son of God. He said we shouldn't be surprised by trials and, in fact, should rejoice in them. And then he suffered and died so that, like the blind man he healed, all brokenness could be redeemed and we could have a true and enduring hope.

Brokenness was healed by Hope. And all brokenness—even the brokenness we presently face—will be a faint memory in our future redemption.

There is something else. When Jesus answered the disciples regarding the blind man, he said God's works are *revealed* in brokenness. Perhaps true hope, then, is actually realized through difficulty and pain and suffering. Perhaps it is in brokenness, when all our false hopes fall away under the weight of grief, that we discover God is strong enough to handle it all. He is able to hold our grief, to accept our questions, and to reach deep into places that no one else can touch to bind up wounds. He is not scared by brokenness; he is revealed in it.

When my sister and I were skating on the driveway or imitating beauty queens, I never once hoped for pain or difficult circumstances. I never imagined that the things I hoped for might actually disappoint or change or be mixed with a measure of the world's brokenness. But I also never imagined that disappointment and struggle would be my greatest lesson about God and about the gospel. I never imagined that I'd see the beauty of the gospel revealed most clearly in suffering.

If you've walked through suffering or disappointment and come through the other side with your faith intact, you know hope. But there are many, including some I know personally, who are currently experiencing deep pain, and hope is nowhere in sight. Perhaps you are one of these people and you are questioning how God could ever be revealed in the hell you're facing. I don't know your specific situation, but I've seen countless situations and this I know: we keep coming back to God with our hands open. That's what the gospel directs us to do: receive. We go to him to receive. We ask for hope, we ask for our hearts to change from bitter to hopeful, we ask to receive what will sustain us. So much of suffering is darkness, silence, confusion, and heaviness. We can't find our way through; we're walking blind. But if we keep going to him in the darkness—not to our false hopes and asking, eventually we'll discover we can see. Our asking—our faith—will have brought us through to hope. Our hearts will have switched and our wounds will have healed when we didn't even realize anything was happening, because we've gone to receive and he's supernaturally given. The gospel is powerful, and in suffering we must give it space to do its full work in us. And the gospel's full work is to show us true hope.

The Greatest Gift

Hope is the ultimate message of the gospel: "Blessed be the God and Father of our Lord Jesus Christ, who according to His abundant mercy has begotten us again to a living hope through the resurrection of Jesus Christ from the dead" (1 Pet. 1:3).

If we are in Christ, we live in hope every single day.

When our son Will turned nine, he chose to take a few friends to Chuck E. Cheese's to celebrate. Mind you, a trip to Chuck E. Cheese's meant an hour's drive each way in the car with six boys, seven if you include my husband, the biggest kid of all. Squeezed between my two youngest in the back row of the car, I heard every knock-knock joke and funny boy-sound known to man.

Will chose Chuck E. Cheese's for his birthday because he wanted to play games, eat cardboard pizza, and earn prizes, but his primary goal was a chance at the Ticket Blaster. The Ticket Blaster is an enclosed tube that blasts air (and tickets) for thirty seconds. Birthday kids get in the tube and, during the allotted time, grab as many tickets as they can. The attendant adds several special tickets to the tube, some worth 50 or 100 points and one ticket worth a whopping 1,000 points.

As Will geared up with goggles and an inflatable birthday crown, his birthday entourage gathered around him to talk strategy. All the kids agreed he should tuck in his shirt and use one hand to stuff tickets inside. Will nervously stepped into the tube, eyed the 1,000 point ticket, and braced for the blast of air.

It came on suddenly, sending a flurry of tickets swirling around him. Inside, he flailed his arms around, grabbing as many tickets as he could. Outside, one of the kids noticed with great excitement that the 1,000 point ticket had wedged itself into the points of Will's birthday crown. At once, the entire group of us stuck our noses to the tube and screamed, "It's in your hat! It's in your hat!" at the top of our lungs. Enclosed in the booth with the blasting air, Will couldn't hear a thing. He continued grabbing at the air, sometimes bending over and threatening the balance of the 1,000 point ticket stuck in his hat. Each time, we would point and scream, "It's in your hat! It's in your hat!" By this time, we were all hysterical with excitement for Will, that he had likely caught the elusive ticket and didn't even know it yet.

For some reason, that moment has really stuck with me. As a mom, having heard Will talk about the Ticket Blaster for weeks leading up to his birthday, I was so happy for him. Even though it was a thirty-second game at Chuck E. Cheese's, it was truly a thrilling moment to watch the other little boys cheer for Will and agonize that the 1,000-point ticket might suddenly fall out of his crown.

But even more so, the imagery stuck with me. I thought about how often I am the one in the Ticket Blaster, hoping to catch the elusive ticket yet possessing it all along.

I'm still, in some ways, wondering if this life of faith will be worth it in the end, wondering if I should be prepared for pain, or if God will disappoint me. I'm flailing around, grasping for assurance that all is well, yet all along it's already there, it's already happening. I live in hope. It's in the proverbial hat!

What I mean when I say this is that I'm a child of God and, as a child of God covered by the grace of Jesus Christ, my position in him never changes. When God looks at me (and you, if you are in

Christ), he sees his beloved child, holy and righteous. He loves us, and there is absolutely nothing that can change that or remove us from his love. Do we sin? Yes. Is God grieved by our sin? Yes, but, by his infinite grace, he is transforming us by his Spirit, helping us realize our salvation. In that process, our position as a child of God never changes.

Those who have put on Christ have been given many gifts, the imputed righteousness of God being primary among them because of our great sin and therefore our great need. Because of this imputed righteousness, we have peace with God, we have access to God, and we escape the just wrath of God. But perhaps the greatest gift we've been given by Christ is real hope. We've been given a grace that enables us to withstand tribulations and to wait with hope for the glory of God to be fully revealed.

We have hope because we've been made citizens of Christ's kingdom, a kingdom we wait for but cannot yet fully see and experience. We hold tightly to our heavenly citizenship because we've been told that, unlike our earthly and temporary hopes, in this citizenship is a hope that will never disappoint or shatter.[1] This is a hope that, though largely unseen, is secure and fast. We can put all our eggs in this basket.

Even better, this is both a present and future hope. It is for this life and also reaches into our eternity.

So it is our present hope in that it enables us to endure trials, without turning to false and temporary hopes that only serve to compound our pain. We can endure suffering because we understand that God is good and just and gracious and that all he does is producing perseverance and character and hope in our hearts. This is hope: that no matter what we face we cannot be separated from God. This is hope: that our sins aren't counted against us because the perfection of Christ covers them over. This is hope: that

From Good to Grace: Responding

our trials are temporary, that death is not an end but the beginning of everlasting joy for those who are in Christ, and that this life is temporary and our life at home in heaven will be permanent.

It is our future hope in that in this life we've been given a deposit, a guarantee of our future, in the Holy Spirit. The love poured out into our hearts by God is a promise that all we're enduring by faith is working for us a far more exceeding and eternal weight of glory.[2] We believe our faith will become sight and our joy will abundantly overflow.

It's in the hat! It's in the hat! Hope is in the hat! I keep telling myself this when I get discouraged and downtrodden, when I turn back to look at my false hopes with longing, or when the enemy speaks subtle lies to me. Because of Jesus, it's in the hat. I can rest easy, leaning on his everlasting grace. It is well with my soul.

Hoping in God

If we are in Christ, these things are absolutely true for us. We have a sure and steadfast hope, no matter what we face in this life. This hope is a noun: a fact, a reality of the citizenship won for us.

Hope is the message of the gospel, but hope is also a response to the gospel. When we truly know noun-hope, it elicits a verb-hope. Hoping in. A choice to reject temporary hopes and embrace God as our one true Hope. Peter says, "Therefore gird up the loins of your mind, be sober, and *rest your hope fully* upon the grace that is to be brought to you at the revelation of Jesus Christ" (1 Pet. 1:13, emphasis added).

Hope is active, directed, and chosen. Peter reminds us that hoping in God is something that requires girding and soberness. Hope, like grace, isn't a sweet, meek little word. Hope is a clinging, a surety of belief, a stubborn refusal to let go. Hoping in God is a conscious choice to place our confidence and trust in God. In

Chuck E. Cheese's terms, the ticket is in the hat but we must claim the ticket. We claim the ticket by faith in Christ, not just for salvation but for our every day.

I have found that what hoping in God looks like is living in my identity as a child of God rather than any secondary identities. I'm a woman, I'm a wife, I'm a mom, I'm a pastor's wife, I'm a writer, I'm a daughter, and I'm a sister. These are not bad things, and I happily fill these roles. However, because my hope follows closely behind my identity, if for example I think of myself primarily as a mom, my hopes are in my children and how their behavior and choices reflect on me. Who am I apart from my children, their activities, and their development? What happens when they don't do what I would want them to do or they embarrass me in public? What happens when they grow up and leave home? If my hope is in them, if my primary identity is as a mother, than I am guaranteed at some point to experience disappointment or loss. I am not intended to place my hope in something or someone other than God, no matter how much of a blessing or a gift many of those things are. We can try to live out of our secondary identities, but this pursuit creates idols and dysfunctions out of good things that are not God.

As believers, we primarily identify as children of God. Because our hope follows closely behind our identity, we then find our hope in Jesus Christ. The foundation of our life is the gospel: that Christ made us righteous through his blood when we were still in our sin and that he promises us a future redemption in our future home. As children of God, we receive, we are served by Christ, and we are led by his Spirit. Instead of identifying as a mom or a wife or according to our vocation, we identify daily with the death and resurrection of Christ. This is our only sure and steadfast hope, and this is the only hope that will never disappoint.

To hope is to stubbornly stake everything on what Christ has done for us on earth and what he will one day do for us in heaven.

To hope is to return to this hope every day and in every circumstance we face.

Paul described hoping as a groaning, a guttural anticipation of something certain that is yet to come:

> [We] groan within ourselves, eagerly waiting for the adoption, the redemption of our body. For we were saved in this hope, but hope that is seen is not hope; for why does one still hope for what he sees? But if we hope for what we do not see, we eagerly wait for it with perseverance. (Rom. 8:23–25)

Hope is based on a certainty that God is capable, that he is good, that he makes good on his promises, and that all things work together for our good and his purposes.

And hope is directed forward.

Hoping Is Eagerly Waiting

When Peter exhorts us to rest our hope fully upon the grace that is to be brought to us at the revelation of Jesus Christ, he urges us to view our present earthly trials through the filter of our future, and draws our eyes away toward the permanent future to come—our future in heaven—that will be free of pain and sin and the pull of the flesh. Just wait, he says. There is a permanent, complete redemption to come. There is a home and an inheritance waiting. The gospel is for our past and it is for our present, but it is *mostly* for our future.

We often don't consider that the gospel is for our future. We don't think about heaven much. There is too much pain, sin, and brokenness to wade through, and the brokenness we live under feels so permanent. But it will, because of Christ's work on the cross, one day give way to the joyful perfection of heaven for those who are in him. A mental picture, developed from Scripture's portrayal, of a future eternal existence diminishes the weight of my daily burden and keeps my hope stubbornly on God.

Now there is pain and heartache. In heaven there will be no more tears.[3]

Now there is sickness and death. In heaven all diseases will be healed and death will cease.[4]

Now we sin and experience the consequences of sin. In heaven we will relate with one another without jealousy, bitterness, hatred, anger, or any other sinful emotion or behavior that hinders us from perfect relationships.[5]

Now we often live in isolation from others to hide our sin. In heaven believers from every nation will live and worship in perfect unity.[6]

Now there are those who struggle with depression and suffer many things. In heaven we will spend our days rejoicing.[7]

Now men and women die or are persecuted because they claim the name of Christ. In heaven the truth will be made clear and Christ will bring justice, avenging the deaths of the martyrs.[8]

Now we cannot see God and we only understand a small portion of his character. In heaven we will be with him and he will dwell among us. We will see him and know him clearly.[9] We will know his love for us.[10] We will be completely satisfied.[11]

This life is passing away, but he will make all things new![12]

The truth is we are so ingrained in the world that we cannot imagine living in a place untouched by sin. We can't imagine complete redemption. We can't wrap our minds around being in the presence of God. We also don't have much of a biblical picture of heaven, which serves to starve our verb-hope and feed our present secondary hopes more than anything else. We tend to think of heaven as an endless church service filled with hymn-singing, where we sit on clouds in isolation from others, suffering an eternity of boredom. In his book *Heaven*, Randy Alcorn paints a different picture:

> I imagine our first glimpse of Heaven will cause us to . . . gasp in amazement and delight. That first gasp will likely be followed by many more as we continually encounter new sights in that endlessly wonderful place. . . . It will be far better than anything we've seen.
>
> Imagine it—all of it—in its original condition. The happy dog with the wagging tail, not the snarling beast, beaten and starved. The flowers unwilted, the grass undying, the blue sky without pollution. People smiling and joyful, not angry, depressed, and empty.
>
> Think of friends or family members who loved Jesus and are with him now. Picture them with you, walking together in this place. All of you have powerful bodies, stronger than those of an Olympic decathlete. You are laughing, playing, talking, and reminiscing. You reach up to a tree to pick an apple or orange. You take a bite. It's so sweet it's startling. You've never tasted anything so good. Now you see someone coming toward you. It's Jesus with a big smile on his face. You fall to your knees in worship. He pulls you up and embraces you.
>
> At last, you're with the person you were made for, in the place you were made to be. Everywhere you go there will be new people and places to enjoy, new things to discover. What's that you smell? A feast. A party's ahead. And you're invited.[13]

Ultimately, our desire, our hope, and our inheritance is God himself: "And now, Lord, what do I wait for? My hope is in You" (Ps. 39:7). Many of the New Testament writers equate hope with our future communing with God in heaven, and they encourage us to keep this hope ever in view.

> For what is our hope, or joy, or crown of rejoicing? Is it not even you in the presence of our Lord Jesus Christ at His coming? (1 Thess. 2:19)

And thus we shall always be with the Lord. Therefore comfort one another with these words. (4:1/–18)

If then you were raised with Christ, seek those things which are above, where Christ is, sitting at the right hand of God. Set your mind on things above, not on things on the earth. For you died, and your life is hidden with Christ in God. When Christ who is our life appears, then you also will appear with Him in glory. (Col. 3:1–4)

There will be a day when we will see his face, when our faith will become sight, and when God's full glory will be revealed and acknowledged. For this, we who hope in God eagerly wait.

Don't Waste Your Suffering

With such a tangible picture of the world compared to a negligible and inaccurate picture of heaven, we do not tend to look to eternity with hopefulness and we don't suffer well. The Bible, though, assumes that being in the presence of Jesus in heaven is such a reward that, in light of it, we will endure any amount of temporary suffering on earth. Scripture calls believers to encourage one another with the hope of heaven, a reminder that being in the presence of our faithful God far outweighs our earthly circumstances.

It is often through suffering and struggle that we learn to hope in God. The Bible says that hope is actually produced from our trials when we see them as opportunities for God's redemption.

And not only that, but we also glory in tribulations, knowing that tribulation produces perseverance; and perseverance, character; and character, hope. Now hope does not disappoint, because the love of God has been poured out in our hearts by the Holy Spirit who was given to us. (Rom. 5:3–5)

To hope in God is to trust the heart of God, that he loves us and that he helps us through the Holy Spirit. It is a belief that he is producing himself in our hearts.

I've learned this most through our autistic son. There are hard days, but God is giving me his heart. My husband and I have a code for our hard days. We call them autism days. *It's an autism day*, I say, and he instantly knows everything there is to know about how I'm feeling. It's shorthand that I'm sad and perhaps a little tired but mostly just sad. It's a sensitive sadness, a familiar sadness, like a wound that's mostly healed and often forgotten, but unexpectedly gets reopened. *Oh yes*, I tell myself, *I forgot. This isn't going away.*

My most vivid autism day happened the week our son finished camp, which in itself is a feat of God's grace and a testament to where we are and where he's come. I went to collect him and his suitcase of stinky clothes at camp, arriving in time for singing and cabin awards. While the entire camp, stuffed into the dining hall, sang and cheered, we parents stood with our noses pressed against the screen windows trying to catch a glimpse of our children belting out worship songs. I found him immediately and marveled as he participated in the hand motions and chants.

The worship leader called out the name of the last song before the campers dispersed for cabin awards: "Lean On Me." Initiating the ultimate Christian camp experience, he urged all the campers to interlock their arms and sway as they sang. Our son's fellow cabin mates enthusiastically obeyed, and he, standing in front of them all, tried to get into the chain of boys, but they refused his entry. He tried again but was denied a second time. Finally, he put a hand on the shoulder of the girl closest to him, who looked at him nervously and started uncomfortably giggling.

His face said it all. He knew he had been left out. He knew it was an awkward moment. He knew he had done something socially wrong, but didn't know what it was. He looked toward me with flushed cheeks and tears in his eyes, I smiled and gave him a thumbs up, though instead I wanted to reach through the screen window and fold him into me.

And there it was—the familiar sadness. I knew I would have to wrestle with it in my heart the rest of the day. Though the song was a small thing and could likely be explained away, those small occurrences and difficult days are like the keys to Pandora's box for me. Pain and suffering take me deep into the recesses of my heart, my theology, my faith, and my perseverance. Autism days provide me opportunities to straighten it all out once again, like ironing out the wrinkles after every laundry cycle. I know I can run from it, wasting its lessons, or I can run to it, letting hope rise again.

On the ride home, I listened to our son's stories about camp, which took approximately three minutes. We played the question game, where we took turns asking each other questions, primarily so I could get more out of him. He asked me trivia questions from our Bible on CD, and I asked him how he felt during the last song. Embarrassed, he said. "Everyone gets embarrassed," I said, and I told him about times I'd felt the same way. "You know I love you?" I asked. "Yes," he said, and then we were silent.

As we drove on, I let him play his coveted video games and I listened to a song that told me God's been wherever I have. The words stood out, but a part of me rose up, bucking the truth of that statement. *I'm sorry, God, but have you really been where I am? Have you parented a child with special needs? Do you truly know what it's like?*

He spoke clearly, with grace and empathy, into the deepest parts of my heart: *I have not parented a child with special needs, but I know how you felt today as you watched your son. I watched as my son was bullied, humiliated, misunderstood, mocked, physically tortured, and murdered. My dear, precious son was rejected before my eyes. I know that sadness and can empathize with you. You do not walk this road alone.*

I remembered then that the Father and the Son were able to endure such difficulty because of the outcome, because of the joy set before them. Perhaps I could also endure or, even better, embrace this road I'm walking, for the joy set before me. Perhaps this road is really producing hope in me, and God is revealed along this road.

I reached to touch my son as my comforted heart simultaneously bowed in surrender to my Father. With hope from a Father's heart, he rebandaged my wound.

An autism day no longer.

Nonetheless, at times my response to talk of good birthed from suffering is a furrow of the brow. It is a difficult pill to swallow. I am, however, reminded by the camp autism day that God hasn't asked anything of us that he hasn't done himself. "For Christ also suffered once for sins" for the good purpose of bringing us to God (1 Pet. 3:18). Paul goes on to give us our response:

> Therefore, since Christ suffered for us in the flesh, arm yourselves also with the same mind, for he who has suffered in the flesh has ceased from sin, that he no longer should live the rest of his time in the flesh for the lusts of men, but for the will of God. (4:1–2)

When we choose to surrender to God and allow his will in our lives, thorns and all, our suffering can be purposeful. It can show the power of God that gives us the strength to say, "No matter what, I am loved. No matter what, God is good."

I personally believe that while we are so quick to categorize pain as a negative, God views it as our opportunity. It is an opportunity for our character to be tested and refined. It is an opportunity to live by faith. It is an opportunity to see God redeem and restore a situation we felt to be impossible. It is an opportunity to experience deep gratitude and joy over even the smallest victories. It is an opportunity to develop compassion for the plight of others. It is an opportunity to influence others and draw them to Christ. It is an opportunity to love with an unworldly, grace-filled love. The opportunities associated with pain that we fear and flee are endless.

When we see pain as an opportunity, the results are scripturally clear. As these verses illustrate, it produces in us a strengthened faith and inner character.

> My brethren, count it all joy when you fall into various trials, knowing that the testing of your faith produces patience. But let patience have its perfect work, that you may be perfect and complete, lacking nothing. (James 1:2–4)

> But may the God of all grace, who called us to His eternal glory by Christ Jesus, after you have suffered a while, perfect, establish, strengthen, and settle you. (1 Pet. 5:10)

> In this you greatly rejoice, though now for a little while, if need be, you have been grieved by various trials, that the genuineness of your faith, being much more precious than gold that perishes, though it is tested by fire, may be found to praise, honor, and glory at the revelation of Jesus Christ, whom having not seen you love. Though now you do not see Him, yet believing, you rejoice with joy inexpressible and full of glory. (1:6–8)

To the cynic, it may seem too difficult to accept suffering from a good God or too simplistic of an explanation that good can come from suffering. But what else do we have if we don't have hope? What else do we have but Jesus?

In the end, we cannot know all the purposes God has for allowing suffering to exist. We cannot see every way that God will use it to bring himself glory. We can confidently trust, however, that any purpose he has is good.

I want to be the person who has honest thoughts and emotions concerning my circumstances but who also has active, unwavering hope. I will never say, "I'm trusting God *because* he will change my circumstances." Instead, I will say, "I'm trusting God no matter what." It's simple to say, but with a flesh that cries out for comfort, happiness, and ease, I have to actively work at placing my heart in this posture of surrender before the Lord. I want a heart that, even when questioning my circumstances, says, *Yes, Lord.*

I did not come to this place until I fled from the goodness gospel, where brokenness has no place, to the true gospel, where brokenness is redeemed. I did not come to this place until I learned to trust in the person of Christ and his heart toward me rather than looking for what he could do for me. I know I'll be disappointed if I trust in God to provide me with only comfortable circumstances, but I'll never be disappointed if I look to God to be the source and object of my hope.

This is hope on repeat: coming back to the person of Christ to gaze on his goodness and receive his perspective, his grace for our daily sufficiency, and his life in us. We so often think that, after putting our faith in Christ, we need to grow in our abilities and in our goodness. We define sanctification in such terms, where we're creating and working toward our own growth. Michael Horton says, "Start with Christ (that is, the gospel) and you get sanctification in the bargain; begin with Christ and move on to something else, and you lose both."[14]

We make it all so complicated when we really only need to return to the simple truths of the gospel and find our identity and our hope in Christ. The Bible says that sanctification occurs as we do this, that the Holy Spirit himself accepts the responsibility of changing us. His ministry to us is life and righteousness. He gives and leads. We receive and respond in obedience.

Over and over. Day by day. Receive and respond. Hope on repeat.

So how do we live in this world while waiting for our hope to come? How do we walk by faith and in grace? How do we put self to death and live alive to God?

At the center of this kind of life is the cross. We can never go far from it because it beckons us to come and die that we might receive, that we might respond, and that we might repeat it tomorrow.

The cross keeps everything in perspective, from our deepest wounds to our darkest sins. When we look at ourselves, we realize that the cross is all we need and, really, it's all we have. We echo Paul's words: "But God forbid that I should boast except in the cross of our Lord Jesus Christ, by whom the world has been crucified to me, and I to the world" (Gal. 6:14).

Our boast is in the cross of Christ and what he has won for us. It is not in our abilities, our goodness, our religious practices, our charisma, our financial statements, our children, or any of our secondary identities or false hopes. It is certainly not in the goodness gospel. We place absolutely no confidence in ourselves, but only in the cross of Jesus Christ.

We also encourage others to look to the cross and put onto it the entire weight of their sin and new life. We don't reinforce the flesh but rather trust God to do the work of sanctification in them, just as he is doing the work in us.

And so we come back to the cross, where grace poured out in the lifeblood of Jesus Christ, where hope was born. Always back to the cross.

Receive, respond, repeat.

Conclusion

We Will Live in Grace

M Y FRIEND SAT ACROSS THE TABLE and poured out her heart, letting me in on the obsessive thoughts of despair and worthlessness that had kept her relationally isolated, wracked with guilt, and so sure that she was a deep disappointment to her husband, her friends, and her God. She could not receive the gifts God offered her—grace, rest, the enjoyment of her children, his strength in her weakness, joy in life—but could only twist them into shame-inducing evidences of her failure. Her sin was so much in view and grace so far out of range that she could only hear condemnation.

"I know exactly how you feel," I said. "I know exactly what you're thinking: Where is the good news in the Good News? Where is the abundant life that the Bible speaks of? Why do I feel so burdened and weighed down by expectations I can never seem to meet? I am a constant disappointment."

"Yes," she said. "Yes!" Her eyes pleaded with me for help, for freedom from her shackles, for hope in her hopelessness. "How do you know?"

I smiled. "I know *because I've been there too.*"

Perhaps you, dear reader, are also deep in the trenches of the goodness gospel and my friend's thoughts are your own. Perhaps you have resonated with so much in this book and the eyes of your heart have been awakened to the realization that the gospel you've believed is a tainted version of the real thing. Seeing the extent of how the goodness gospel has pervaded our lives can be both confusing and overwhelming, because trying to right the ship with truth, we know, will throw all of life into a tailspin for a time. *I know because I've been there too.*

How do we respond when the goodness gospel is what we've built our lives upon but we want to tear out that false foundation?

I will tell you the same thing I told my friend: putting off the goodness gospel so that you can know and believe the true gospel is a process much like re-wallpapering a room. You must tear down the old wallpaper—the lies you've believed about God and what he expects from you—and put up new wallpaper of biblical truth. As anyone who has chipped away at old, stubborn wallpaper and wrangled glue and sheets of unruly new paper knows, it's often a messy and time-consuming process. But it's worth it in the end to bask in the beauty and glory of the new, just as it is to rest in the peace and joy that are born from the gospel. *There really is an abundant life to be had in Christ.*

The first and best thing you can do is go to God and say, "Teach me about you. Show me your heart and help me understand what lies at its core: love, grace, peace, and joy. I know nothing of these things." Doing this opposes the self-sufficiency that you've lived by in the goodness gospel. Doing this puts God in the rightful place of change agent and serves notice to your flesh. Doing this invites the Holy Spirit to do what he does best. And nothing gets

God more excited than his child approaching him with a desire to know his true character.

You can't climb your way to grace, so don't go with your natural tendency, which is to be in charge of your own change. Let him be in charge of change; let him be in charge of the process. Rather than claw your way to him, simply fall back into him. This is where the receive/respond paradigm begins.

God *will* lead the process of sanctification as you present yourself and your questions to him and to his Word. He *will* reveal himself and what is and is not true.

Soon after giving yourself to God and to the process of receiving and responding, you'll discover that living by grace requires a daily focus on faith. Faith will be the glue for the new wallpaper to go up and stay up. God will show you his grace and love, but you must choose to believe him in order for the truth of the gospel to sink deep down and then well up in response.

This isn't splashy faith. This is day in, day out faith that works in the mundane just as much as at the point of salvation. It's a focus on process rather than immediate results. I think we're all drawn to the idea that our life should be full of big splashes for God, perhaps because we think that is what pleases him. But no, what pleases God is faith—that we believe him when he says that he offers us grace, that he loves us, and that he can be trusted. "But without faith it is impossible to please Him, for he who comes to God must believe that He is, and that He is a rewarder of those who diligently seek Him" (Heb. 11:6).

For our purposes, we must also believe that God is not in the business of daily performance evaluations. Condemnation is not from him, and we must learn to turn off the voices in our head that tell us otherwise. For this, we will again need the Word and our faith, because Scripture tells us that good behaviors are not what he treasures most; what he treasures most is faith. "For we through the Spirit eagerly wait for the hope of righteousness by faith. For in Christ Jesus neither circumcision nor uncircumcision [good works meant to earn God's favor] avails anything, but faith working through love" (Gal. 5:5–6).

God asked me a long time ago if I'd die for him and I'd thought of martyrdom in a foreign land, but he'd really just asked me with gentleness and grace if I would die to myself and to the goodness gospel to which I so tightly clung. His call was to the cross, to know and believe that Jesus had died and risen again, and his call was for me to die so that I might rise to a new reality of redemption, that I might receive. Today's call is the same and tomorrow's also: lay yourself down and receive. Receive and enjoy God and let the floodwaters of his love compel a response.

I may just be doing 416 loads of laundry a year or listening to a friend in need, but I know for sure that this is a life that matters in God's kingdom. A purposeful life, I've discovered through the gospel, is not oriented around a one-time event or a mind-blowing work that draws the attention of others. Those were the thoughts of a young, inexperienced girl. A purposeful, impactful life is something much simpler than that, something I can wrap my mind and life around, something we all can wrap our lives around and give ourselves to.

It's the gospel, and the gospel answers our questions—What does God want for us? What does God want from us?—with great clarity. He wants our hearts, he wants us to receive what he's poured out, and he wants us to let his love overflow our heart cups and spill out onto others. *Love.* All of the law is fulfilled in that one word.

We want to be good—good spouses, good parents, good friends, good workers—but we see in light of the true gospel that this is a destructive pursuit. It is also a pursuit of what we already have. We are enough, because he's made us enough. We're righteous and holy, because he's made us righteous and holy.

So we root in what's been given. We receive what's been given.
We *respond* to what's been given. We'll never go back to our pitiful, man-made goodness gospel, thinking it can give us life. We
know the truth: Christ is our life. We will live in his grace. We are
grace-dwellers, and this is our manifesto that we will return to
again and again, believing it by faith:

This is the gospel: not that we are right with God because of what we
do but that we are right with God because of what Christ did for us.

The gospel can be twisted so easily, and we have believed the
lies of the goodness gospel. It has whispered so convincingly that
our salvation was a gift received and the rest of the Christian life is
up to us and whatever effort we give it.

But we will be fools no longer; we will not pursue what we already
possess. We won't be debtors, and we will not give our lives over to the
fruitless chasing of goodness and image and religious plate-spinning.

No, we will not be obsessed with goodness; we will be obsessed
with God. Instead of dictating to him how he should be honored, we
will give ourselves to what he says are the most important things:
receiving from him each day and letting his love and grace compel
us to worship and to love and to serve with joy. Our external actions
will mirror and flow from our internal affections.

We believe that God is a singing God, a celebratory God, and that
he delights in us. We release our grip on our own agendas, ambitions, and dreams of self-glory so that our hands are free to receive
his love. We refuse to stiff-arm the truth of God's love because we
feel unworthy. Christ stands in our place, and God loves his Son,
therefore God loves us.

We know that the Christian life is impossible on our own merit. We
can't love sacrificially, forgive easily, or obey joyfully without someone
leading and helping us. And so we don't walk in self-sufficiency but
rather we depend on the Holy Spirit, our Helper, to lead and empower
us. We practice spiritual disciplines as a means of asking for his help
and leadership.

We identify with Christ, and our true home is built with the bricks
and mortar of grace. Because of his grace, we are free from thinking

too much about ourselves and free from thinking too much about the opinions others have of us. We make it our aim to please God alone.

Assured of God's love, we are compelled by him to love others. We participate boldly in the community of the Beloved, where we sharpen and are sharpened, and we go as Sent Ones to share the love we've experienced.

Assured of God's grace, we give grace to others, with the goal of unity rather than uniformity. We trust God to lead us all, and we know that sometimes he leads us differently on open-ended issues. Different is quite beautiful, so we use our differing gifts to show off the beauty of Christ and we champion others as they use theirs.

Assured that we possess the greatest treasure, we turn from false hopes that only compound pain and suffering. We fix our eyes on Christ and run hard the race he's marked out for us. In our trials, we give him our hearts, letting him produce in us character and perseverance and an enduring hope.

In all these things, we live and die and live again, all by Christ. We do not allow ourselves to be entangled again with a yoke of bondage. That makes Christ nothing. We stand firm in grace's freedom, where Christ is everything.

Acknowledgments

JESUS, THANK YOU FOR GRACE. Thank you for redeeming me. I love you and hope you are honored by my words. They are meant to be a response of worship.

Kyle, aside from Scripture, you are the one from whom I've learned the most about God. You consistently show me his love and grace. Thank you for your unfailing support in my mothering, ministry, and writing. I am so glad you're my husband. I love you.

Will, Reese, and Luke, you remind me often that, by getting to write a couple of books, all my dreams have come true. I nod and smile, but in my heart I'm just thinking about how you three boys are my real dreams come true.

Thank you to all my family and my friends who have prayed for me and encouraged me in life and in the writing process. I see God's grace demonstrated through you and, because of that, I understand it better and love him all the more.

Acknowledgments

Coming to an understanding of grace is my ongoing life story. I'm grateful to the wonderful people at Baker Books who have given me the opportunity to write this book and share what has most shaped my life.

Thank you, Les Stobbe, for your spot-on insight and for helping me navigate the publishing world.

Discussion Guide

Chapter 1: Obsessed with Goodness

1. The author asks herself, "Am I a good Christian, wife, mom, and minister?" Do you often question whether you're good at your roles? How would you know you're good at them?
2. Do you feel like you're waiting for the day when you're "good enough" for God to use you?
3. The author says there is a disconnect between Jesus's message of abundant life and our everyday lives because we're striving toward goodness and we're driven by the expectation of what our lives *should* look like. Do you agree? Do you sense this drive in your own life?
4. Do you struggle with feeling that you're not doing enough for God? What would it look like to live a life that's pleasing to him? Does it involve more activity or more faith?
5. The author calls her striving for spiritual perfection the "goodness gospel." Do you see evidences of the goodness

gospel—guilt, self-focus, pride, a muted understanding of God—in your life?

6. Referencing 2 Corinthians 5:21, what is the true gospel? How is the true gospel different from the goodness gospel?

7. According to Galatians 5:4, what happens when we live by the goodness gospel?

8. How would your life be different if you lived as if the gospel were applicable not just to your salvation but to your everyday?

Chapter 2: The Most Important Things

1. The author uses the analogy of frantic hospitality to describe how we are often busy in good activities but miss the heart behind why we're doing them. She says, "Through my good works and activities and service, I dictate to Jesus how he should be honored. Working myself up into a frantic, over-scheduled mess, I just grow burdened and weary and do not love anyone or anything." How can you relate?

2. Do you hear the message of the goodness gospel: our spiritual growth is up to us? Have you recognized it as the goodness gospel or do you have trouble discerning it from the true gospel?

3. The author says the goodness gospel permeates our Christian culture because we're asking the right question—"What does God want from us?"—but we're asking it of the wrong audience. We're asking anyone and everyone *but* God. Do you tend to go to others for answers to this question before you go to Scripture?

4. How would Scripture answer these questions: What does God want *for* us? What does God want *from* us?

5. Self-sufficiency feels so right to us, but what does the gospel really say about self-sufficiency? How do we kill self-sufficiency?

6. What are some of the immeasurable riches found in Christ? How did we get them?
7. How would your life look different if you received from Christ each day?

Chapter 3: You Can't Go Back Again

1. After having received our new reality of redemption, why do we so often return to spiritual self-sufficiency?
2. Why is it so important that the gospel be proclaimed to us? How do you proclaim the gospel to yourself or have it proclaimed to you?
3. How have you seen the goodness gospel affect you or others?
4. Read Colossians 2:20–23 and discuss why the goodness gospel is so attractive yet so powerless.
5. Discuss Colossians 2:6. How can you apply the truths of this verse to your life?
6. Discuss the attributes of the goodness gospel. Do you see these in your own life? How does the true gospel speak to each of these?
7. What is written on your ID card as a child of God?

Chapter 4: Receiving His Love

1. As a child invited to God's table, what kind of guest are you primarily: bringing a good-works casserole, cowering in the corner, focusing on serving rather than relationships at the table, or joyfully receiving the Host's love?
2. The author says God is a celebratory God. Do you agree?
3. Do you think of yourself as a saint and as a member of the Beloved? Why or why not?

4. Does it make you uncomfortable to receive from God? Is your instinct to jump instantly to response before receiving from him? How does John 13:8 address this?
5. What is God's love like? Use Scripture to help defend your answer.
6. Did the description of Ruth and her spiritual slavery give you any new insight into God's love? If so, what?
7. What does it mean to be redeemed *for* God?
8. How is God jealous for us?

Chapter 5: Receiving His Help

1. In the author's words, "We walk around like it's up to us to figure things out and get things right and finally get our lives in order." Can you relate to this statement?
2. Have you ever considered that, if we choose to do it on our own, the Christian life really is impossible?
3. What kinds of messages have you gotten about the Holy Spirit? What do you know about the Holy Spirit? What do these Scriptures say about the Holy Spirit: 2 Corinthians 3:5–6; Galatians 3:2–5; 5:16–17; Titus 3:5? What other Scriptures can you find that help you understand the Holy Spirit?
4. Why is the Holy Spirit so important to us as we reject the goodness gospel?
5. What does it mean to rely on the Holy Spirit in our daily lives?
6. How do we recognize the Holy Spirit's leadership in our lives?
7. What is the proper place of spiritual disciplines in our lives?
8. What is our necessary response when the Holy Spirit leads us?

Chapter 6: Receiving His Freedom

1. What does it mean that, as Christians, we identify with Christ?
2. How do you regularly identify yourself to others? How do you inwardly identify yourself? Do you give these identities too much value?
3. How does grace free us from being self-focused?
4. Have you experienced grace freeing you from trying to please people? If so, how?
5. The author says, "When we compare and compete, we tell lies about our Father." What are those lies?
6. We have genuine feelings of fear from knowing we're not enough for God. How do we apply grace to our fears when our feelings overshadow truth?
7. How does receiving grace and resting in what God has done for us go hand in hand?

Chapter 7: Love Shows

1. In the author's words, "If we receive [God's love] as he gives it, we *will* respond to it in some way, because God's love is compelling." Do you agree? Can we trust God to compel us and enable us to love?
2. Discuss 1 John 4:19. Is this a statement of truth about God's love or a command to love or both?
3. Read Galatians 5:14. How is all of the law summed up? What, then, is the most important focus in a Christian's life?
4. How do we show our responsive love to God?
5. Why is God's love the motivation for joyful service?
6. Do you practice the cyclical pattern of service: receiving from Jesus, responding by loving and serving others, recognizing your inability to sustain love, returning back to the One who can sustain you, and receiving once again?

7. How does the gospel free us to love others?

8. It seems that God often redeems our weaknesses and past failures as a means for us to connect with others. Have you found this to be true? Could you share an example?

9. What is your participation as a member of the Beloved and as a Sent One?

Chapter 8: Giving Grace

1. The author shared what she learned in her marriage: "Different isn't wrong. Different is just different. And different is even quite beautiful." How does this apply within the Body of Christ?

2. When is different *not* okay? In other words, what are issues that Christians should be united on?

3. Read John 21:15–22. What can we learn about Jesus from Peter's response?

4. How does the practice of the goodness gospel create division in a church?

5. Have you ever felt "lesser than" about an open-ended issue? Have you feared talking about these issues with other women? How might you approach your next conversation with another woman in a grace-filled way?

6. How has God gifted you to uniquely display Christ in your family, workplace, church, and/or community?

7. Do you give grace to others in how you think about them? Why or why not? If you struggle in this area, how does thinking about the extent of grace Christ has given you change your perspective on others?

8. How does one live free but also with concern for others?

9. Why is it often harder to counsel other women with grace than it is to counsel them with law?

Chapter 9: We Hope

1. What are some of the false hopes you've had in life that have ultimately disappointed you?
2. Why does the goodness gospel not hold up under pain and suffering?
3. How is God revealed in brokenness?
4. When you consider the current pain or disappointment you're facing, the gospel doesn't always offer to change your circumstances, but it always offers hope. What is our true hope?
5. What does it mean to verb-hope? How do we verb-hope in the midst of trials, especially when we instinctively want to run to easy and false hopes?
6. The author says that our hope follows close behind our identities. Does your primary identity correspond with your greatest hope?
7. Do you hope for heaven? Why or why not?
8. What does the author mean when she says, "Don't waste your suffering"?
9. How can you begin to practice the theme of the book, "Receive, respond, repeat"?

Conclusion: We Will Live in Grace

1. Discuss the grace manifesto. What might you add to make it personal for you and for what you want to remember from this book?

Notes

Chapter 2: The Most Important Things

1. 2 Corinthians 5:21.
2. Romans 1:18.
3. Romans 2:4–5.
4. Oswald Chambers, *My Utmost for His Highest*, classic ed. (Uhrichsville, OH: Barbour Publishing, 1963), December 17.

Chapter 3: You Can't Go Back Again

1. Michael Horton, *Christless Christianity: The Alternative Gospel of the American Church* (Grand Rapids: Baker, 2012), 121, 130–31.
2. Rose Marie Miller, *Nothing Is Impossible with God: Reflections on Weakness, Faith, and Power* (Greensboro, NC: New Growth Press, 2012), 4.
3. Galatians 3:1.
4. Colossians 1:13; 2 Peter 1:3; Romans 8:11.
5. Galatians 4:19, emphasis added.
6. Galatians 5:1.
7. John 6:28–29.
8. 1 Thessalonians 5:23–24.
9. 2 Corinthians 11:3.

Chapter 4: Receiving His Love

1. Romans 1:1.
2. Romans 1:7.
3. Ephesians 1:6.
4. Galatians 5:1.
5. A. W. Tozer, *The Pursuit of God: The Human Thirst for the Divine* (Camp Hill, PA: Christian Publications, 1993), 9–10.
6. Romans 5:8.
7. Romans 5:10.
8. Romans 5:9.
9. Romans 5:11.
10. Big Dream Ministries, *The Amazing Collection: Kingdom Books* (Alpharetta, GA: Big Dream Ministries, 2004), 77.
11. Ibid., 78.
12. 1 Corinthians 15:34.
13. Ephesians 2:7–9.

Chapter 5: Receiving His Help

1. Galatians 5:18.
2. 2 Corinthians 3:17.
3. Galatians 5:22–23.
4. Romans 8:1.
5. Galatians 5:16.
6. 2 Corinthians 5:5; Galatians 5:5.
7. Romans 14:23.

Chapter 6: Receiving His Freedom

1. Colossians 2:15.
2. Timothy Keller, *The Freedom of Self-Forgetfulness* (Chorley, England: 10Publishing, 2012), Kindle edition, loc. 333–34.
3. Nancy Wilson, *The Fruit of Her Hands* (Moscow, ID: Canon Press, 1997), 53.
4. C. S. Lewis, *The Weight of Glory* (New York: HarperCollins, 1949), 29–31.

Chapter 7: Love Shows

1. 1 John 4:19.
2. Hudson Taylor, *Intimacy with Jesus* (Littleton, CO: Overseas Missionary Fellowship, 2000), 17.

3. Ibid., 17–18.
4. Ann Voskamp, *One Thousand Gifts: A Dare to Live Fully Right Where You Are* (Grand Rapids: Zondervan, 2011), 192–93.

Chapter 8: Giving Grace

1. Hebrews 12:1–2.

Chapter 9: We Hope

1. Romans 5:5.
2. 2 Corinthians 4:17.
3. Revelation 21:4.
4. Revelation 21:4; 22:2.
5. Revelation 21:27.
6. Revelation 21:24.
7. Revelation 19:6–7.
8. Revelation 2:9–11; 19:2; 20:4.
9. Revelation 21:3.
10. Revelation 22:4; 21:2.
11. Revelation 21:6.
12. Revelation 21:5.
13. Randy Alcorn, *Heaven* (Wheaton: Tyndale, 2004), 17–18.
14. Horton, *Christless Christianity*, 62.

An Invitation

DEAR READER, I'm so grateful to have explored God's grace with you in this book. We've dipped our toe into the ocean, have we not? Let's go in deeper! You're invited to join with me and other grace-divers as we learn what it means to receive from God and respond to him in our day-to-day. Come find us online at www.GraceCoversMe.com.

Christine Hoover is a pastor's wife, a mom to three energetic boys, a speaker, and the author of *The Church Planting Wife: Help and Hope for Her Heart*. She enjoys encouraging ministry wives and helping women apply the gift of God's grace to their daily lives. Christine's work has been featured in *Desiring God*, the Gospel Coalition, *Christianity Today*, Pastors.com, and in(courage). In addition, she offers fresh doses of biblical truth and grace on her blog, www.GraceCoversMe.com.